A Familiar Shore

EMILY ISAACSON

A Familiar Shore

TATE PUBLISHING
AND ENTERPRISES, LLC

Published by Tate Publishing & Enterprises, LLC
127 E. Trade Center Terrace | Mustang, Oklahoma 73064 USA
1.888.361.9473 | www.tatepublishing.com

Tate Publishing is committed to excellence in the publishing industry. The company reflects the philosophy established by the founders, based on Psalm 68:11,
"The Lord gave the word and great was the company of those who published it."

Book design copyright © 2015 by Tate Publishing, LLC. All rights reserved.
Cover art: Long Beach, Tofino by Tatjana Mirkov-Popovicki. Used by permission.
Cover design by Junriel Boquecosa
Interior design by Mary Jean Archival

Published in the United States of America

ISBN: 978-1-63306-710-3
Poetry / Canadian
14.11.28

To Miriam
(August 19, 2013)

The botanist is the master who leaves their signature on the civilized world.

The virtue of the candle lies not in the wax that leaves its trace, but in its light.

—Antoine de Saint-Exupery

The head of the statue was made of fine gold. Its chest and arms were silver, its belly and thighs were bronze, its legs were iron, and its feet were a combination of iron and baked clay. As you watched, a rock was cut from the mountain, but not by human hands. It struck the feet of iron and clay, smashing them to bits.

—Daniel 2:32-34

Only ask, and I will give you the nations as your inheritance, the whole earth as your possession. You will rule them with a rod of iron and smash them like clay pots.

—Psalms 2:8–9

The Huron Carol

'Twas in the moon of winter-time
When all the birds had fled,
That mighty Gitchi Manitou
Sent angel choirs instead;
Before their light the stars grew dim,
And wandering hunter heard the hymn:
"Jesus your King is born, Jesus is born,
In excelsis gloria."

Within a lodge of broken bark
The tender Babe was found,
A ragged robe of rabbit skin
Enwrapp'd his beauty round;
But as the hunter braves drew nigh,
The angel song rang loud and high...
"Jesus your King is born, Jesus is born,
In excelsis gloria."

O children of the forest free,
O sons of Manitou,
The Holy Child of earth and heaven
Is born today for you.
Come kneel before the radiant Boy
Who brings you beauty, peace and joy.
"Jesus your King is born, Jesus is born,
In excelsis gloria."

Translated from Wyandot language
by Jesse Edgar Middleton

Contents

Preface

Embroider the Sun Across the Sky

There was once a beauty who lived in the heavens. Her name was Iron, and she wore a path across the sky with her journeying. Her cloak had the sun and the moon embroidered on it, and she had hair as dark as iron, and eyes of ruby fire. She wished for everyone in her company to be happy and full of mirth—but she tortured anyone who was sorrowful or downcast by pelting those with hail when they were most frightened. At times even a meteor shower descended on her enemies. The place where she lived was a formidable palace in the constellation of Andromeda. She was known as the Princess of Ethiopia.

In Andromeda, the palace ramparts were made of ebony, and the floors were teak and marble. The princess had many layers of clothing, all of silk, made right in her palace. Of course she was extravagant, and every detail was attended to. Her table was a banquet every night, at which the Andromeda stars would dine. As they came in from the night sky, their white hair shone, and long beards touched the ground. She consulted with their wisdom night after night at her grand table. The stars were the oldest beings in the galaxy and knew the wisdom of the sands. The glittering dust that fell from their shoulders was moon dust, and their eyes shone like the blue embers of a fire, for they were prophets.

Finally, after much deliberation at the banquet of the princess, speaking in murmurs of candor far into the evening, the stars considered their revelations. They believed that the time was drawing near when the people of the earth, who were guided by the horoscopes and influenced by the constellations, would turn back to the baby born in a manger in Bethlehem. They would ignore the wisdom of the Andromeda prophets and revoke their influence. They would even fight for their freedom from their bond of slavery to the night and its visions from the Princess of Ethiopia. For if they dreamed her dreams, or heard her torturous invocations, they would turn against all who sinned and bring them low to the earth—that they might never walk again in the land of the living.

Iron was full of the horrors and the atrocities of mankind, and that is why she could pelt any young woman to death with universal stones for any subversion, or test a man's heart by buying his rights to die for his country with a death of patriotism, while others stood by as only helpless victims. Iron was quick to take a person's sense of honor and duty and create a spirit being within them that would look down on all who did not uphold their morals. In fact, they might even be led to commit a crime of honor.

The stars of Andromeda concluded that a young woman had been born on earth, and that she alone had a song that had been given her by the angel to be sung into the dark night of the soul. She would be a minstrel trained in music and gifted in lyrics. She would wander over the northern earth and find a forgotten and abandoned people—recreating them as mighty men of valor with purpose and leadership.

The Princess of Ethiopia was boastful at this revelation.

"She shall not outlive me, for I am immortal," she said. "Nor has she the power to convince men from their moral religious ways to kindness. She must be poor, or I would have heard by now of her royal birth. But I shall listen to the movement of the celestial bodies and see if what you say is indeed true."

With that, the furious Princess of Ethiopia ascended her stair to the tower of the iron empire observatory and kept watch over the night from her telescope. She was never one to admit the possibility of defeat, but she knew it had happened once long ago when a young songwriter and shepherd boy had met a giant and flung a smooth stone from his sling. When the giant had toppled into the dust, Israel was victorious. Could this young minstrel and lyricist have the power to invoke such similar feats?

About the same time, in the constellation of Aquila, there was an empress named Clay. She was unique of valor and lived in a palace of crystal. Here she taught the many constellations in her school of directives to life each day, what is right and of virtue. She was a noblewoman, and she took the form of an eagle. In this form, she circled in the sky over the north during the time of the clay empire. She was a predator and gripped the salmon from the mighty rivers as her own for nourishment. She was solemn, unlike a statue, but glassy and fragile. Without rain, she would crumble into the dust of the earth.

It was in the moon of wintertime when Clay first sighted the First Nations People struggling to eat and live over the Northern Hemisphere. They were put on reservations of land, but without her help, could not survive the cruelty of humanity nor the cold of snow and ice. This people were often poor and had only their pit house fires for warmth. Clay decided to send them a messenger named Sea, with her child, Rain. Sea came forth from the ocean one day, toddled onto the sand and began her life. What she called forth, prospered, for she was a poet. Her child, Rain, watered the garden of the earth. Her best friend was a minstrel, who played the titanium flute. Now we shall hear their story, as a ballad of old.

The Moon of Winter

Stars Grew Dim

In the days of Galileo, there was a hierarchy among the stars.
I thought she would rule an empire; she was
strong, when fortitude was of the essence.
She was iron royalty. This is what I knew
about the Princess of Andromeda.

There was a healing from the clay when
the Messiah walked on earth.
He fashioned it with spit between his fingers.
A ray of light descended on the road of compassion.

Andromeda

I.

The gold gate of unrequited love swung on
its mighty force, freedom in its hinges,
looked on a barren, lifeless sky
and called it forth to birth—
of our tears and reckonings,
these existential galaxies of fiery
beings, these stars, forgiving velvet
in a city of knives, warming souls and
bringing with them the evening
and all its worth. The Princess of Ethiopia,
with a word, drew her iron empire to sleep.

What light came into darkness, woven
a subtle embryo, swimming in ocean clarity,
the womb a canopy over banquets
bold, fragrant food and wine, colorful fruit
spanning the year-long table, differences
in a myriad of forms, put aside;
the artist wept, his paint plural, in black dress
from ways of society, and genre—
staring out over the handsome rye fields
stark against the prairie dust, cultivation
a metaphor of strong stable marriage.

II.

My existence on earth had become
more mythic than concrete:
I sat at my table, lit by a single candle,
and painstakingly embroidered
each seashell in the tapestry of the shore.
I was the sea, and the ringing
tide's familiar devotion,
its dependable crash of waters,
the spray of salt, and the wild game
of nature all embedded
themselves in my consciousness.

There was a courage to begin,
the monumental task of drawing a map
within the human soul—a diagram of life,
pertaining to freedom
from conflict, abuse, and stigma.
There was a standing,
eyes fixed, hands outstretched,
with a fury to equal the storm,
and a calling to water the shores of nations.
To be not just one
but many faces, thoughts, and emotions.

There was always a way of love and a way of hate.
From the very beginning the stars came
under the Princess of Ethiopia
or under the Eagle.
Those who loved soared with the eagle,
those who hated were controlled with an iron rule.

What of the very dust of the earth when it is brittle and dry?
Could we not repent and our tears soak from
the sky, making wells in the desert.

Antlia

I.

The planets of our conscience,
carved and creviced with silver years,
revolving 'round the deed of our suns
with creaking restraint of the air pump;
moons of our descant want
enticing us from our beds,
to gaze upon the light of night.
Yet we tend toward resolution
of our wrongs. The silence of waiting,
the brokenness of wings that can no longer fly.
We wait for restoration, as the morn.

What breath peeled dewy morning from sunrise,
shadowing lilies of the ancient path,
neat gardens specked in red and white expanse,
skirts of dancers twirling on the smooth lawn,
flawless bright comment of the early sun,
the wind of heaven lent its full perfume,
when I heard the following of birds
descending from steeple mount, larks, sparrows,
seeking the reflection of the green's eyes,
darting over all that is paradise—
resplendent as honor from the lost sons.

II.

I feel the character
deep within my mind,
of the oceans and their elements:
the waters of the earth
belong to a queen—
she is regal and trustworthy,
she is the mother of one child
whom she adores, as an equal.
Rain is her child,
she dampens the people of the earth,
sowing their seed within the ground.

Rain bears a divine name,
carrying waters close to the heavens,
she is of a true nature,
telling life with honesty, beauty, and pattern,
she is dependable,
appearing again and again
in the seasons of the earth,
she is the sustenance: flowing rivers
and passing streams,
the flooded scarlet cranberry fields,
the fruit of harvest.

One's own soul was his charge, and his
standard reflected the honor of nations;
yet death comes to all, and all must
pass through its iron gates.
Here one would find that he had
triumphed or had failed in misery.
For triumph is the greatest of all gains.

When I asked a question, it lingered
until the answer was found.
For an aged universe must search out the answer
to riddles in its book of knowledge.
And an intelligent man must speak simply
until he is regarded as a simpleton, so all might understand.

Apus

I.

The tropical green was a shade of virtues
that had not grown dim, the exotic bronze calls
of the bird of paradise echoed through
the universe, with a tapestry of lights
and shadows revolving as pencil-marked grace notes.
Deep within the stars
of its pattern, were the gems of valor,
dictating the beauty of returning
to home, the softened light, and the fear of emptiness.
Yet death's requisition!
Aloneness, before their cameo onyx God.

What thistle rooted self in the conscience
of man, a thorn, embedding itself
in human flesh, an unfamiliar pain
and requisite suffering, hollowing
his eyes into a vacant stare, inane,
the trivial, a competition in
improvement—and weakness, avocation.
We decree our ordinance to conserve
all that remains, in one declamation
embodied by the hills we left behind,
the insult hunger, too heavy to change.

II.

I stretch out my hands,
the waterways of the world,
shaded canals of Venice,
river of the Amazon,
the royal Thames, the straight-limbed Nile.
How did I come to be
the speaker of the sea,
the voice of its relentless pull
and heartfelt rhythm.
My initials spelled sea,
I contained it—

Wild and unrestrained,
fettered and monopolized,
used and bettered,
the sea was my portion,
the Queen of Water.
I was as much
a victim of the moon,
as a mother in labor
is subject to her pain.
I knew the rites of nature,
the turning of the earth.

What wonders of love, breaking on the spiels of time. How it came to be that I was the architect of the human race, a strong and stately woman of virtue, was a story of its own. For when the deep rang out, I answered my doorbell.

The visitor was an old watchmaker.
He had wound up the seasons of nature,
and left them ticking in succession.
I watched from my window. It seemed indeed true
that he had made us to be independent
of him but not of his love.

Aquarius

I.

The aqua water bearer grew as a melon
under the earthen sod, a rounded lump
beneath the surface of the galaxy,
when bursting forth, with fresh and
seed-filled succulence, was harvested
for an evening meal, with ham
and potatoes au gratin, the wine glasses
chilled, a Sterling Merlot.
We sat and stared over the heads of our guests,
the table set with linen napkins, and
carved elephant napkin rings.

What plunder was a force of position,
distinction between sides, copper faces
flourishing like a parade, peering through
the backbone streets, plethora of sainted
stammers shafting and plunging contagion
with deliberating style and pomp.
The spare and unprolific old despoil,
ransacking the scenery to tainted
color, expressing pride without symbol,
conspiring to daring heroism
by some, and analogous silent traits.

II.

I wrote all day and into the evening
with a sharpened pencil,
sketching the notes of my composition,
floundering in its depths,
bringing my emotions
back from death to life,
as a killer whale returns to surface
from the undercurrents of the sea.
The words that would create
are the words of a healer
and the healing.

These words embody the power of nature
to restore its essence,
to remove impurities,
its resonance to similitude.
They thunder within the galaxy
of the cell, the microscopic layers
of mitochondria; they storm over the sea
before the nucleus of the sun.
The sky each night
grows dark with nutrients,
then silent with solitude.

The will is a strong force that will shape a person,
a future, and even a nation. Who would reduce the
strength of human resilience to broken eggshells.
When we are fearful, we have forgotten our destiny.

The teacher of the school of directives to life was an eagle
who rewarded penchant for observation.
For a prophet is an observer of human nature,
and seeks to understand why people act outside their beliefs.

Aquila

I.

Drawing forth waters from the heavens,
the rain followed on steady iron wings,
bright with rapid lightning, and the thunder
of rebellion. The school bell echoed down the hill,
yet a boy kept hidden under the trees,
ignoring the call to stability, for the open
country, for freedom like the sea.
I looked out the window at the empty
grounds, over the rows of heads bent,
studious over their work. When it was time
to sing the anthem, only one voice was missing.

Why was my figurehead
etched upon a coin? The touch piece
was a keepsake and currency of a nation
emaciated and gaunt,
starving for the food of my voice—
resonant and luminous as the fruit of the vine.
My charger went forth, no more than a colt,
yet I was a horsewoman.
What I could not imitate of the ardent prayer,
I swallowed and said again in my own words,
opening the heavens and descending like an eagle.

II.

A child's mind,
the necessary fluidity and flexibility
to comprehend the unending
verses of science and nature—
in a war of lilies, between
the gilded and the wild.
When my back was turned,
my child conducted
the strings, the woodwinds,
and the brass;
her sincerity was stunning.

She had a look of complexity
and musicianship,
her dress from the undergrowth
of the woodland was that of a oil painting.
She was strong and lean,
subsisting on blackberries
and wild game.
In the city, I found her
with a bow and arrow,
hunting a prey that should
be only in a deep wood.

The choir of elements, hidden beneath the earth, reinforced
this witness. The resounding stillness of sunshine and
reddened leaf, of snow and new blossom was sealed.
Each season came forth in choreographed silence.
The demarcation of time grows subtly as the rings on a tree.

The enterprise of barricading the door was
the opposite mission of coming to earth.
Placed in a manger, in the form of a baby,
this young child would grow into a man,
could mold clay to make a universe of unrequited love.

Ara

I.

The sacred mind, of virtue and its
innocence, the small white lamb
on the altar of sacrament, and one
wistful thought, that life in all its beauty
did not disappear as a fading wind.
We thought of the times we
had spent sprawled on the lawn
before the mighty cornfield, row upon row,
drinking our iced tea, over poetry,
with biscuits and sandwiches. Until the fall, when
the desolate cornfield was ploughed into the ground.

What was too fragile to hold on, the wing
of a clay butterfly in flight was love,
ponderous and riveting, hungry, bold—
taking a canvas by surprise without
paint or artist, just a smash of glass parts
doubling back on all that was victory,
jubilee of visions casting shadows
that extended far into the parking
lot of a garden you would pay to see.
The gravedigger came by with a shovel,
faulted me on leaving a single rose.

II.

What would my child say
in an urban myth,
where the lights of the city
decorate the darkness
and stars grow dim?
The various instruments,
unlike differing languages capable of words,
were examined and their possibilities
for the order, and catharsis of music
over sound's cacophony
brought a familiar reassurance.

My child Rain hunted for words,
writing solemnly as words came,
slowly at first, then in tempered staccato—
fishing in the river across the road
for symbols, as salmon from the arms
of a reassuring mother,
flipping a coin for the reasoning
that came only in riddles.
Her mind was clear as morning.
*Shall I ask for directions
if I am lost?* she thought.

Color is most winsome when it is passing through. The kinetic iris interpreted the moments of light and shadow as the moments when virtue prevailed, or loss and fear dictated. For a dictator seeks to subdue obedience with terror and articulation with insult.

There is a road of reparation, and those who travel
on it find peace and forgiveness. The clay of the
road bears his footprints. The fruit of the tree
he passes by is his constellation of seeds.

Aries

I.

The ram appeared in the heavens
and the old man pointed by night. Galileo
would initiate us with the gold-studded invisible,
refractory in having a certain
infallible surety that the abrupt,
cramped and homely bonds of earth were seared at
the sun's imprint—and he indicted,
to his dishonor and imprisonment here,
where all who see the star cross the heavens
abide. Our aching limbs and passiveness,
traded for lifeless immobility among the dead.

Surely a defense was allowable,
for what court would now again
insist insight cross over the earth?
In definition, the world continues on,
poised and enigmatic,
with unfailing tenderness
and gratifying conclusion.
Its universal course—aware,
in painstaking clause, of the familiar
announcement and engraving
of elegy upon the grandfather clock.

II.

The minutes ticked away,
the author continued her discourse,
and the wind and Rain obeyed.
There was a hush,
without blinking of eyes,
as the child and her mother stared
into the deep midnight
of the divine iris.
There was a hue the size
of a dime, and it grew deeper.

There formed a rainbow:
the colors that the divine iris refracted
were stayed in forty shades,
penetrating and impervious.
They contrasted
the black and white
of former worlds,
of newsprint,
of courtrooms,
of textbooks, examinations,
and concentration camps.

I took the hand of a child once and guided her through
a galaxy of meteors and unsubjugated fire. The beings of
heaven have much more understanding than the scavengers
of earth, for they are as old as the universe itself.

To commit perfection is to commit atrocity, for the far side of perfection is death, and the beauty of our acceptance of all beyond our control reaps unselfconscious stirrings of the imagination.

Auriga

I.

Where was my faultless heart?
When roaming—the charioteer—through the rays
of vast and desert moons, barren and dry,
did the spirit find in me a place to rest
and corrupt for the purpose of the accused?
I resisted its notion, praying instead for the pure
and perfect, sinless symbol of restoration.
I am incorruptible when I am pure metal,
found as an ore in the side of a hill.
Evil chastised me to a fault,
but I resided in my power.

Where was my riveting soul?
The silver laugh that made me a person
had disappeared when I adopted
a skeletal frame, with the intent to die young;
but youth hath ransomed me back
as the rose on the vine,
and the sky pierced by thorns—
the tumultuous storm
hath pealed its lightning,
tenuous as a vision in winter of a lineup
of black faults etched, then buried beneath the ground.

II.

I am human,
but when I write
I am the sea and my child
is the Rain—I sketched
in pen and ink,
a formidable task
of writing legend
and resurrecting fable.
The urban myths
became more than
a cup of coffee over the news.

They were urban mythics:
a predictable force, timed to the minute
like the clock faces
of old, first a sundial
formed of slanting shadows,
then a ticking in unison
of several time zones,
then the realization
that all society must be aligned,
in every country, with
its gestational second hand contractions.

So the countryside is laid waste with foliage in decadent
hues of Gregorian color. The multicolored panes of
the stained glass window emerge from the stone.

When each soul is ransomed from beyond, there is an individual turning back from all that would lead to destruction. When I am set apart for a purpose and future, I dare to stand alone.

Bootes

I.

The suffering induced by the bear driver
that had seemingly no solace,
dark night of the soul,
the point of no return would take me captive.
Even so, there remained the beauty of darkness
interspersed by a radiant navy.
There was an ethereal light around the streetlamps.
I walked home from the train station.
I began to hum Barber's *Overture*.
I pulled my rabbit fur hood closer
around my face, and my eyelashes froze.

What was my character's resolution?
The unquiet was bronze and choleric,
the open space replaced by horses and carriages,
old roads, and stores with forged business.
I bathe drenched in the rain,
I ask for meaning when there is none;
the water streams down my hair,
outspoken that we are natural beings
marked by time and the passion of gods:
nourished to a science
and not without fruits and flowers.

II.

When I paused from my work,
I gazed down at my multifaceted
utilitarian diamond.
It spoke of a commitment
to something of the eternal,
infinity rambled on
as a horse would plod
day after day for its master,
without indebtedness,
only the trot of dependability
and the canter of gratitude.

The page, in its almost empty
form was a canyon
I must fill with the sunrise
and the last light
daily, in anticipation
only of death, not of life, for I was
unlike an ancient tree—waiting for,
yet unable to die.
The fear of nothing,
was a fear of trading
evaluation for acknowledgement.

I bound my hair of autumn and cleansed my
winter skin, then fashioned saints in living color—
right from the beginning to the end of time.

They were a canticle of living virtue. Bowed in prayer, they kept each person in the center of the will of God.

Caelum

I.

The sculptor's chisel stayed poised
in the heavens, with a bust of marble
still in midsentence, the head of a woman
appearing with white eyes of immobility,
hair streaked with fine powder,
and the mouth of gentrification.
Her words seemed trivial and inane,
the density of bone an enigma
of her statuesque form,
the notes of theory before her
as a cookbook for the food of angels.

How did I set a fine banquet?
My philosophy was an ideology in copper
that chastised many as a scourge
above the realm of earth and its archetype;
the olden tree shall not now slay me—
no curse shall rest in me,
I yet secure a deeper tree.
I shall live and enlighten
the dark with food and wine,
new each day—a carved table
at the elaborate end of time.

II.

The vase of my soul,
once overflowing with the flowers
of praise and encouragement,
was suddenly shattered
into a thousand pieces:
the crystal scattering
of the stars far into the night,
of the jellyfish into the sea,
near almost invisible—
yet brightly gleaming
with iridescent beauty.

There was a purpose
in the chaos, the disorder
between the minds
of a man and woman
who said—I love you,
I hate you.
It erupted into universal violence,
storming as a hurricane out of the sea,
flooding the river into the chiseled
façade of the city and quaking
the roots of Haida Gwaii.

There was first a word of pardon, then the healing of the wound. First there is the asking, then the receiving. The old Gregorian melodic line rises and falls as the breathing of the human chest.

The healer knows the intricacies of life and death, and the decisions that make wholeness resound through every minute cell. So she might make one drink the bitter remedy to discipline the inner man. When he is headstrong, he is drunken and not infatuated with integrity.

Camelopardalis

I.

I set out as a healer,
to make women strong
as the giraffe dancing in the desert
beneath the iron light of Africa,
where the midnight tribes
search for the light of constellations
to guide their way. I evoked a medicine
that would not wane and would not leave.
It buffered the starvation of the poor
with the alkalinity of a plant-based constitution,
all with the silk of white baking soda.

What was my constitution?
Bright, and glorious as a warrior in arms;
radiant and celebrated for a medium and a cure.
My modality of the natural earth, and its healing
was eminent, resounding
on the waves of mental anguish,
retribution to the wounded generation
that refused to hold on and jumped,
blinded by the architecture of the famous and noble,
their characters dishonored—
not the womanhood I used to know.

II.

I took up my favored pen,
and the meter of the salt roar,
the splendid gathering of stony shells
and aged driftwood
splashed off the pages
of the handmade paper, enameled
with rose blossoms and leaves,
for the retrieving of countries
almost lost
in the density of ocean,
for the salve of a wound time has marred.

The earth quakes
beneath my feet at this final hour,
the nations part ways
with reason, and many
are refugees under a molten sky,
swollen with sadism.
The pewter drops of invisible
Rain are the only respite
from death that raps
at the door, demanding
its children be put out in the cold.

There is the coldness of the human heart, which
sheds its cloak in heartbeats, and the breathing
truce that life must continue. Then there is the
tearing away of a bandage from an old wound.

Waiting for healing is like waiting for a
messenger in the night who brings good news,
or an aloe plant to grow by the sea.

Cancer

I.

The ocean licked at the feet of my father,
storms reflected in his grey eyes,
he taught us to hunt for food beneath
the salty depths, first lowering a cage
to capture the sunset-hued crustaceans the size
of a man's hand. We five children
sat in a row and gratefully ate our crab-meat salad.
In late summer, he picked wild berries by the pound
to store up for the winter and hunted island deer.
The wild game began to run—would I be pragmatic
or reflect the gifts of my father. For he asked:

"To what did I bow down?" In enmity I was imprudent,
sacrificing too much of myself for clay of no value.
Know the reason you were born.
Sell nothing for a coin for money cannot buy a soul.
Reap what you would invest,
and destroy not your education on lesser things.
Work only at what you would do for no pay,
without asking for a reward.
Don't ever beg for spare change like an outcast,
but plant your tree as an olive orchard
in a fertile valley of old Israel.

II.

There were two prophets
beneath my hands:
the sea and the rain.
The ocean was unlike
a salt sponge, dotting
the crevices of earth
with lapis color.
All seven seas lined up
as bridesmaids, escorted
by the continents made of limestone,
carried on an elephant's back.

The bride swept her high beams
across the highway of outer space,
piercing the night with a moon-faced
candor, riveting planets;
solemn, the groom waited for dawn,
then came forth
in the chariot of the sun.
His light was so breathtaking
that she faded into the invisible
until he fell asleep. This is why
men sleep under an enchantment before beauty.

In perfection we are lost, as there are only witnesses of true suffering. The planets reel in contrasting notions to site-specific reality where there is only one answer for every question.

When I am alone before the Creator, I suddenly realize that intimacy is about adoring wholeheartedly what we have together that is not shared by anyone else. I know that one day I will face you alone, and who I really am will be the person you knew all along.

Canes Venatici

I.

The hunting dogs descended on the falcon,
and the dark-winged horses followed
the blare of the horn. To the ends of the earth
and back, to covet a single oath
not to draw back when duty called,
my staid chore was balancing the fierceness
of the forest wood with the Anglican cathedral
choir, the remedies were prolific in kind,
yet cruel in their absence. We must not
fester malignantly, but walk the benign road
of reparation. I raised a toast, "To restorative justice!"

What was my maxim? For what did I live
and for what did I perish? Beneath a gold crown,
were my waistlines eternal, and did my neck,
surrounded by jewels, as a night
places the gemstones of planets, moons, and stars,
draw a crowd?
Did the fawning nation swoon when
I came out, restless
as an immense sea roaring at the composed moon
over its correction and manipulation,
harsh as the salt waves, euphoric in my mouth.

II.

As I am permitted to write,
so the sea is permissive
to the shore, allowing it to
draw up a will, pending its death
upon the next rock or island cliff.
Yet the shore's familiar logic flounders
in the face of the great injustice
of humanity. Its anorexic hunger
spends itself in the third world
searching for water,
its seeds withering in the heat.

Here, women pour life's last
oil into jars and wait for prophets.
Here, the well is dug, after
great sacrifice.
Much support is gained
in the observation of how
one could not feed oneself,
and lay motionless in the dust,
forgotten of the world's
happiest people—they trusted
in their ivy-league educations.

At the sanction of realized
achievement is a worthy cause.

Each moment spent in contemplation,
repeats itself in the spirit,
as the continuous waves upon the open
sea reverberate to the shore.

Canis Major

I.

I was white as ice, platinum cold, then dark
as a wintered landscape with a hedge row
of bitter holly, a recollection of order.
I looked on society, no semblance of
the selfishness of wealth without generosity,
nor of the bruising of poverty's
pitied face in want.
When my appearance was no longer idolatrous,
my very shallows blasphemous,
I will have taken a quill and ink
and composed the verse of kings and queens.

In what spirit did I rule?
When I spoke words of silver,
what resounded into the room
was swimming and submerging
beneath the waters of a river
no one could cross.
I buried my face in the dust,
I offered my cheek to my enemy,
never passionless or indifferent
my motions carried into deathlessness
at a banquet whereupon death would dance.

II.

I was a mountaineer of the highest Everest
when the rain became a misted cloak,
sodden on my shoulders,
dredging the grave behind my back—
for all who had fallen on the steep paths,
never to return. Yet they climb day after day,
for a man is wild at heart.
A woman in Africa
must depart every day for water,
bringing it home to her household,
carrying the russet jars high upon her head.

The unicorn of the sea
was opposite the sea lion;
the long horn of time beckoning
as the circular gleam of a light house,
casting hope before each ship
to safe harbor. I stood before
the rocky shore, bested by triumph,
and a great artist stood before me
at his easel. He repainted me in colors
of the sea, so I would find my place
in the museums of humanity.

When the sea was a field of the deep,
each word was retrieved
as a treasure from a sunken galleon.

Rebellion is a masked attempt at
happiness without the rules.
An archer always aims to hit his target.

Canis Minor

I.

I had a handful of hemp hearts,
the oil of which protesters
knew no bounds in decorating;
the rough sewn clothing, a dramatist
in the collection of numbed desires,
smoky pain and curbed rebellion.
They tested the marketplaces of earth
for more buyers, found medicinal
uses for the drug, and enlisted a colony
to populate Mars. We stood in line,
expecting loneliness, only to be turned aside.

Where was I found?
The bronze meadow was my home,
the gem of seas, all seven,
the Bear Mountain I knew
like the back of my hand,
the solace of the lace of the fields
I gathered into the hem of my garment.
I touched the waters of meribah
when I drank from the crystal decanter
and forged a way through the wood
for a people: my nation.

II.

The sea has such joyful sailors,
but without lemons and oranges,
such depths of sorrow.
To each man who walked the plank,
there is a credit of mutiny.
Mutinous is the 'morrow,
for it entices a man into slavery
beneath a fickle sun,
with no hope of a savior;
to the glory of each sunken galleon,
writhing in gold doubloons.

We search the face of the deep
for a call of God,
to bring us the benefits of life,
the bounty of offspring after us.
Yet she is a woman
walking through gestation and birth
of both kind and unkind alike.
She is the desert in its pangs of hunger,
and the waters flooded with mercy.
She is a home for the wicked and the good,
her life is neutral in resonance.

Winsome moments pass from you to I,
the taking of hands with the present for nature or
nurture: a dotted meadow of buttercup lace.

When I sent for the pattern of this meticulous work of art, it was in understanding that it would take many hours for it to be accomplished. Embroidery was always slow and time-consuming, with many colors.

Capricornus

I.

The apples and raisins of my breath,
throughout the future of the long secret—
as the poignant shadow that falls gladly
on a crowd friends when the sun has passed.
The still-life marketplace was a fruit bowl piled high
with pineapples and coconuts, with spice sticks:
cumin and cinnamon. I stood stock still
and let strangers pass by me, surmising my wealth
from a single basket of the sea's bounty.
I fled on horseback to the next town, doing only
what I knew of servitude to freedom.

What was the meaningful open question,
kept like a memento of the copper powers that be,
presiding over autumn ground
such as wide fields, ditches, and mossy barns
where no one could hide. No sound could be heard.
I hear the call of my child's voice again, resonating
as tears on a statue, marble in cream,
tenuous as a violin's ransom,
the vision stark at nightfall, dispersing
faults of the self and inner world, image
painting the character of eventide.

II.

My pen was silent at this thought,
for it must be my final hour on earth
if I have been given the wisdom of sages:
yet it was all contained from the first
in the waters that gave birth to my spirit.
When the early structures of the earth became stable,
I was the architect at your side.
My scarf collected the gleanings of your fields,
my head was anointed with your oil,
as an olive tree's fruit
blackens and is sent to the oil press.

The mission fig hangs in space
as a darkened sun,
when I sliced it down the center,
it contained pockets of calcium.
They sustained the bones
of the poor, nourished
the unwed mother and her starving child.
The widow and the orphan
stop at the door for food,
we blacken the bread with molasses
to feed their charred souls.

My worth was poured out,
and I repent in oil and vinegar.

The constellation of beans and corn circle in my warm soup of the galaxy. I am lost in time, and remember the days when the moon was like an unbroken gourd and guided the way.

Carina

I.

When I am contrary to perfection,
I am human in the eyes of God;
when I am contrary to virtue,
I am a victim without embellishment.
Never have I seen
the ways of children,
without the deciding powers of what is fair,
nor spent the dreams of my life
in becoming tenanted by fires
in the night, yet it is this fire
called to lead a promised people.

What was my lady?
The statue was iron-silent, beckoning of power,
yet elegant in infertility,
a lament with an ode to the sons and daughters
of others, bleak and illustrious—
reflecting honor as a mirror
that would leave us unconfused as to the distinct
separateness of a mother and child.
The figure held a similitude, measuring time
and distance with a tape measure
instead of a scale.

II.

A blaze would come forth
from these ashes,
burning the very soul of the city of knives:
for the women of the day
knew not the men of the night
and their god anarchy.
The chaos knew no bounds when
they torched the city to destruction,
dancing in their fires of torment.
The mainland city was scorched
and suffering with debris.

This place off the sea coast, Vancouver—
wind ruffling her hair off Granville Island,
where the theatre is open
to the crowd, and the market piled
high with fruits, olives, and oil dressings.
Here a savior could appear unannounced,
win back the hand of a young woman
with ankle-length skirts and long hair
named the minstrel. They called her to play.
She faced the sea. She had turned
her head long ago, and knew the charges.

My will of iron could not destroy unless it was
bound with clay, and then it shattered the earth and
leveled the temples of doom. It tore up the fields,
and houses disappeared beneath the wind.

My tears would fall unnoticed into the earth, for I was a traveler who read the sky by night and the times by day. No one would feed such an eloquent apprentice with anything but light and shadows.

Cassiopeia

I.

The craving for perfection
is a craving for death.
In the destruction of all
that is imperfect lies
the true death of a soul.
I had no soul; my spirit wandered here and there,
purposeful as a person without body
could be, with no attributions
for all that was of dignity
could never be mine, with no likeness
to a human form.

Where did I break, and fall into the heart of the sea?
Why did the chasm open to swallow me like clay
deep beneath the earth,
infusing me with the gems of nations,
and their varied colors.
I found meaning in the little things,
and recorded the symphonies of nature.
Somehow the movement of the shadows and lights
over the earth, played like a chord
upon the harp, its stringed note lingering
into the dust of mankind.

II.

As long as the minstrel faced the grey waters,
she was not neglecting her calling
or her compatriots. Her ballads
sold for a pretty penny, and the melodic voice of
her titanium flute rose above the crowd
at the art institute.
In sheer disbelief, the long line of theatre goers
paused at the sight overhead.
A conglomeration of seagulls moved in subtle
pattern, assembling in the hundreds.
They flew high and low, reveling in the music.

She was right, that the harp was a somewhat
ancient instrument, rather like a Stradivarius—
with nothing its equal. The soft plucking
drew each gull in and out of a concentric universe.
Unlike stars reeling and planets turning,
the gulls metered the air,
plunging through thought and emotion
so she was a David to her Saul,
soothing the affliction of the city with a harp.
There was a lament, that reminisced all the way back
to the gates of Old Israel, when Rachel would weep.

Wandering Hunter

Colored panes belayed the light, and images
of the saints tiptoed in the quiet.

While there is a moment to celebrate, there is also a moment to deliberate on what is the best way. When one has ascertained the spiritual, it makes sense to climb the ladder of angels.

Centaurus

I.

In the flower shoppe,
the peeling red roses—
startling of love
from barrels in corners—
asking for respite in desperate voices,
writing on note cards in spidery scrawl
the quiet to steal heart after heart;
a subtle perfume, dense and aromatic,
as you were, the colorful bouquet,
woven dexterous
by angels.

The dark comes at the end of each evening,
blotting out the transgression of former hours,
piercing through our sin are the stars.
They compared me once to a night without stars.
In all her journeys into the soul,
a woman gathers her power,
as nature recreates itself each day.
Summoning all that is within her,
she imparts strength to those she loves
and those she must forgive,
writing them notes with flowers.

II.

I worked part-time as a florist,
whilst writing volumes of poetry,
my pen scrawling notes in the background.
The sea and the rain would never actually
part ways, they just kept giving back
from what they had been given.
One lapped at the pilings in White Rock,
as we walked to the end of the pier;
the other poured from the sky on rain days,
we did not open our mouths to catch drops
as we would when we were young and uninhibited.

The minstrel's children
were at the top of every street,
she wept when she saw
their needle-marked arms, heard of the
fallen leaves of the Downtown Eastside.
She took out her guitar, applied a capo,
and began her haunting descant:
"Will I have loved
if I do not love the poor?
Will I have loved
if I do not love the hungry?"

One cannot be a gardener and grow a weed. Every flower is precious, and has a name and color. A weed must be torn out and burned upon the fire.

Somehow when we leave behind what we love for worship, it is as the mighty men, leaving the ones they love for war. There is a time and a season to fight for what you believe.

Cepheus

I.

In the garden, when it is time to harvest each bloom,
I fill my apron with the orange blackberry lily,
red hot pokers attract hummingbirds,
the flowering maple sighs,
and the pot marigolds are impish suns
against the grail of slight and beguiling
butterfly weed—moderate and sparing.
The table vase overflows
like a storehouse of grain, the reward of the rich
who have time on their hands,
the omission of adversity.

A vagabond could not make me miserable,
for he rambled through, and called me not to ally
the sweet or aged compound
that delicate swans would enter
as a modest qualification for flight.
We were bashful and grieved
after fumbling unguarded
through rows of recompense,
counseling our hearts
not to feel after awhile.

II.

When I decided to become a writer,
I did not count the cost.
I did not know I would feel pathos,
that I would be practicing my pirouettes
for six hours a day
like a dancer in the Royal Ballet.
The search for a word,
its beguiling reason, a thought
no more than a floret or bud
promising bloom—yet all within
my soul held the promise to create life.

Words of life: words that heal.
I watched Rain from my window.
She had gone out into the garden to play
in early afternoon. Her favorite thing
to do was make mud pies.
I stood in the kitchen in my apron,
and watched the apple pie bubbling in the oven.
I knew when dinner was served,
it would be potatoes and peas,
with an iron metaphor—just enough
to generate pause in the conversation.

An artist aligns his subject on paper to his
truer essence, using color and light.
Our first impression of this masterpiece increases its worth.

An olive tree is the place from which virgin oil flows. Each olive hung on a tree once, ripening in the sun. Black and lithe, they strengthen what is weak and fortify what is broken.

Cetus

I.

Growing beside the road,
the yellow sunflowers, flecked with seeds,
belay the superfluous
practical song
of a tall, lithe, and lanky youth
hanging over you, quietly
scorning each vase
as petite and transparent;
so, I time each brush
and align each subject
with respect to God.

Painting each petal
of the bold, didactic day
with both light and shadow,
and finding the furrow
from which it sprang—
invisible until appearing here,
upon a canvas that stares me down
with the fury of silence,
the lover's quarrel, invisible,
appearing and disappearing
in a forte of unrepentant love.

II.

The pause of midday,
the hush of the crowd
left room for a young man
to begin speaking.
He held out his hands,
they were untouched by
the etching of pain, neglect, and abuse.
Yet he carefully saw
the analogy between himself
and the broken,
in an old churchyard symbol.

They wanted him to repent
of his perfection,
to mar his body and scrape his sores
with God as his witness.
He claimed to be as an olive tree,
took only olive oil as his food,
his tears coursed
as oil down his smiling face.
So the crowd of addicts called the art gallery
to send out a sculptor
to chisel a statue of the perfect young man.

As iron rusts over time, so the human body moves toward decomposition. All the universe unravels toward decay without the steady hand of the botanist.

The essential oil of rosemary is the anointing of faithfulness;
when one embarks upon a journey of life, one chooses
the continuum that will bring the most fulfillment.

Chamaleon

I.

The spirited garden, welcoming light's trance:
the energy of green arugula,
the spicy aftertaste of kindness,
all are harvested in summer in the vegetable patch.
Enterprising young women
grow their efficiency with their survival
instincts to feed the whole family,
bringing the nourishment richly
from earth to table.
The diversity of colors
speaks of prevention of all illness.

Before imbalance takes hold,
there is a lessening of the anguish
that comes with being alone, of being lost,
of being abandoned, for the higher
image of being together,
being loved and being cherished—
until the love that cherishes women
will build them a home in the wilds of soul.
The balance returns, enigmatic;
and women are whole again, when they trust
in the wisdom of their bodies, sheltering their souls.

II.

The wild game began
where I knew the minstrel
would see in the young man
a saint—for he loved the poor,
and they hated his perfection.
So the minstrel played them yet another song
about a young saint who walked
barefoot in the snow.
His footprints were so warm with love,
the snow melted.
His name was King Wenceslas.

The crowd's coldness melted like snow.
A poor man came in sight,
collecting matches. Now,
the young man named Wen
spoke of his eucalyptus oil,
how it anointed him
with the sign of the cross,
and prepared him for his work.
For eucalyptus was both cooling
and soothing—a cleansing
balm for the sick and hurting.

The work of centering a person to love with
unselfconscious desire—is one that laughs over
mistakes—the rider of a well-trained elephant.

The hallmark of the flower market, is that love is eternal and must be consummated by the continuity of commitment and the essence of the rose. Each lover buys his loved one roses of desire and rubies of devotion.

Circinus

I.

I knelt down beside
the ice blue clematis,
digging in the flower bed
as a child would;
the regal voice of the delphinium
was a navigator through the seeds
I captured from the rough dry pods
of other worlds,
far as a bluestar bloom—
watercolor print,
blurring figurative color.

We took our brushes, dipped them in water,
as the communion of a mass
celebrated in lofty perfume
without the dark earth
to anchor us in silence,
refining our gaze
over troubled grasses,
tumbling through innocence
to the emporium, where
bouquets are purchased en masse,
each guarded to its depleted wilt.

II.

The minstrel let Wen
converse with the poor
while she played,
for his oil was not only his protection
from pestilence and filth,
but also his ministry unto God.
She knelt down on the pavement
as she played the guitar,
each chord a lament against
the evil that had befallen these real humans,
leaving them chastised in the street.

The minstrel's beautiful lyric,
emanating new from one day to the next,
always drew their emotions
from restless to still,
exchanging their desolation
for the employment of understanding.
They heard her coming each day
from a distance,
stopped and turned their heads.
Wen, fragrant as a sunrise,
heard their pain creaking as the lepers of old.

The hideous awakening of every person's
carnal mind is the moment they realize
that they can't have what they want.

When healing a disease, every minute is
precious, and every word counts.
Joy is of the essence, and forgiveness is a remedy for the ages.

Columba

I.

If I had a house,
I would grow the purple morning glory
in profusion along the white picket fence,
bearing blooms
like the saucers of teacups,
holding the steaming aster,
profiting from the wake of dreams
like the foam oft the sea-born shore,
lashing its May night salvia
in a tumbling low vibrato of selves;
the wind, rippling her sleeves in operatic earnest.

I introduced the afternoon
to its late slanting rays
warming the grass and cooling the shade.
Divided between hot clasps and sipping cold ices,
the visitors would draw lots
to play croquet
with red, blue, and green mallets,
breathing impassioned circles
across the construed terrain,
a seasonable game
with varied opportune endings.

II.

I sat at my cherry wood desk,
pausing only for supper,
writing into the evening.
My script was in ink,
whimsical and spidery.
The minstrel had played
all day on Granville Island,
then spent several hours on the Downtown Eastside,
plucking the harp and singing
her songs in the night
right on the street.

Wen had decided to give
their autonomous duet
of chant and speech
before the poor and addicted
on the Lower Eastside,
the name of "The Gregorian Minstrel."
Wen dedicated their work together
from the boardroom of
his multi-million dollar mansion in North Vancouver,
he was the heir of his father's estate,
and refused to play golf on the weekends.

Similarities between children are seldom of notice,
yet every adult must be uniform and congruous.

We would rather give into our joys than our sorrows,
for fancy is fleeting and melancholy
disrupts the continuum of lifelines.

Coma Berenices

I.

Where we traveled onward,
there was a collection of brown velvet bulrushes
their tips piercing
through whispers of morning
and rippling infernos of late heat,
silencing the objections to pure design,
swaying bold and tall
with an ear to the scoria
of the roadside,
their apathetic anorexic duty—
to move the doctrine toward graceful.

I touched raw limpid ground
where I walked for three miles
without getting dusty or skirts torn,
allocating the day by minutes,
waiting for an exception
from discomposure,
rumpling my cloak,
the look forever of abandonment
running as a fever under the
truce of nostalgia, seasons changing,
the mountain staying evertrue.

II.

"When we are rich, then we are poor
in God's sight. He has sent the rain
to fill the seas, to water the earth—
and he has sent us the poor and hungry to feed.
When we are as orphans,
without a home, God takes us in—
the mother and father we were meant to have.
We are not common,
but royalty, adopted as sons and daughters."
Wen seized every moment to evoke emotion
from the fray of homeless with vacant eyes.

They sat on the curbs, in smoky
wisps, with faded jeans.
Looking to light their fires
with his kindling, the addicts of the
Lower Eastside began to crowd
the parks where Wen stood
to address them after
the minstrel played her colorful
tunes and entrancing rhythms
on the titanium flute, harp, and guitar.
For she played at no cost.

A Lodge of Broken Bark

Raven and the Sea

Only one person need speak into the silence.
Only one dreamer must have the dream.

We dream ourselves into existence.
All planned growth, skill, and activity
have their being first in the dream world,
somewhere in the dead of night.

Corona Australis

I.

After the herbs are harvested,
the black wild rice is poured, mingling
in a pot of boiling water with all that is vapor—
a voice sounds above the boiling soup,
asking for human rights
to extend to the natural man
and his holistic medicine, dispensed
in silence and contemplation,
the cure for an ill that had no name,
just a painting on the wall
with no author.

I would look at the physician
and be amended to
for all that was not right on earth.
I would be right to a fault
if it would heal disease,
creating a distance to surpass
all that was committed.
Pushing my aching limbs to the limit
of endurance, and testing
my own faith
until vexed or perplexed.

II.

Somehow, I ordered my days
according to the time I had been given;
I was diagnosed with inoperable bone cancer
when I was only thirty-eight years old.
I stared at the wainscoting of the wall
for two hours. Surely this could not be,
I thought desperately.
The minstrel was my sworn friend
in this world, and her bright, seeing green eyes
had not predicted this unfortunate outcome.
Yet, I was determined to make the best of it.

I decided to finish my latest poetry volume
and travel to Ucluelet and Tofino for a break,
to be comforted by the sound of the sea
at Long Beach, where stragglers
visited the realms of a familiar shore;
where artists hocked their art
for coins along the wooden streets.
I had visited there many times
as a child, and knew the beaches
and trails far into the wilderness of soul
would be healing for my condition.

To indifference is the mind callused,
for the wells of compassion,
like the deeps of the sea, are unlimited and crash
onto each new shore with juxtaposed furor.

Consensus is the art of making the
discrepancy between two viewpoints
a simple matter of collaboration.
Rhetoric speaks so as to convince a crowd in its favor.

Corona Borealis

I.

In the last days,
the white climbing iceberg rose
reached heaven
where there was a choir of decisions
abated only by a master of the storm,
his calm evoked a decrescendo
over the lake;
his reply silenced a subjective crowd
into tumultuous objectivity,
the potter's wheel of moist watery medium
turning light into music.

My theory, the tap tapping of the conductor's baton,
dividing grace note from semitone
and rest, the accent of passion,
the quarrel of indifference designed to touch
dissolution, until we fall again like molten clay,
revolve around the sun,
as planets on axis would.
The humanity and divinity of art,
fingering matter, word, and texture,
as an army waving surrender
to their mortal enemies.

II.

The calloused face of an eagle's cliff home,
jutted into the sky, covered with moss,
overlooking the sea.
Children wandered by,
stirring the sand
like a soup of
salt water, clams, and seaweed,
calming the horizon with their silhouettes,
beckoning to the tide.
The eagle soared overhead,
white wing tips brushing clouds.

The children gazed upward,
as the water of the ocean
sucked onto the sand,
then drew back
with foamy whispers.
They murmured among
themselves, while
piling the sand into turrets.
Then the sea would come
when they had left
and wipe the slate of sand clean.

Maybe this would be my last day on earth if
the world was mortal and could shatter;
but should I reach heaven, I would be ashamed.

My memory of character was of being utterly convinced
that someone was more real than I.

Corvus

I.

The bold stems
and the clear perfume of the Maid of Orleans,
fill an apron with sweet tender petals,
the perfect flower of the conservatory,
reveling in the hush of amazement
subtle as the voices of angels,
the feathering of wings surrounding
a high-strung temperament without languor,
the mission whispered
in hushed tones to a priest,
both of unity and dissonance.

The barely discernible canon
was an eclipse between sun and moon,
a truce when her disquisition
showed its allegiance
leading to her confinement and restraint
as the sea within its bounds;
the maid prayed to God.
Fervent, she leapt from the tower,
escaping with no malice,
with a widow's peak in her forehead
until the nation stood at the gates of unrequited love.

II.

The language of the seashore
was broken
as the rugged grey rocks
and brittle pieces of left-over shells.
A white mist hung over
the froth of water,
and I sat on a beach chair,
my auburn hair rustling in the breeze—
writing painstakingly with a pen and notebook
into the afternoon, out of reach
of my sworn enemy, death.

Her long dark braids
hung down her back.
The young native woman
was a peculiar sort of girl, with dark eyes
and a political mindset,
as she deliberated the weighty
flood of the tide with pageantry;
her thoughts were neither
fruitless nor unprolific,
examining the evidence of what
would be her verdict.

When one person commits error,
the next person follows him
and then the next, so as to normalize
the first wrong decision.

One cannot ever be a dancer part-time.
If one dances, it consumes all one's life,
every waking moment with the next arabesque.

Crater

I.

In South Africa's rainfall region
the late autumn flowers of the pink belladonna lily,
an expensive and hardy
fling in the sun—
or advertisement for terror,
dappling temptations as waves of heat;
a dark cloud lay at five over the city streets,
soup in various flavors
was spooned to the hungry,
before they turned on their lavish host
as a screaming and inebriated riot.

She stands alone
with her back to the crowd,
she sang this song once before,
her black hair like a field in the wind,
the resonance of her voice
startling and dying away
on a horizon,
weathered by doubt and fear
of beauty or nothingness,
as the castaway clothes in bright hues,
rifled with poisonous dyes.

II.

The native girl's command of the elements
reached a crescendo as I scribbled on paper—
as birds pillaged the stinging shoreline
of mussels, salted threads
of bladderwrack, dark purple,
and plucked beneath tiny rocks.
Finally she took her mace in hand
and decided to confront the sea
directly, padding on in her tiny
worn moccasins, to the water's edge.
The salt tide roared in turbulence.

She, both amiable and zealous,
only spoke: "O forbidding sea,
who once cared for the elders
of the First Nations People
with both nourishment
and harmony, I am Raven.
Of the moon's weighty feat,
and the sun's bright heat,
you are lofty in the mansions of the deep."
This she spoke, translucent,
while the waters crashed at her feet.

What salt can cleanse will rise again.
A wounded prophet must wait until
the false has passed him by,
to take hold of the true constitution of being favored by love.

The unity of thirst in the desert comes
from the indifference of mirages.
When I step into an oasis I am in love with the
tangle of voices and the birds of paradise.

Crux

I.

An atonement in artistry
for the vainglory of early spring, peach blossoms
filling the countryside with blush nectar;
I count my blessings
like a hummingbird counts blossoms,
returning again to the gifts
of authenticity and unity
with restoration in my open hands
sitting at the tables of communion
with a circle of friends,
with the old and young.

The elements of wind and rain
was an idea she sketched on paper,
tasting the damp foggy morning
with the cream she stirred in her oatmeal,
beige as linen.
Humming in perfect pitch,
a purist of sound
like the quality of a note
from the bird in a wooden cage,
and she peered into purity
through the bars of her wooden gate.

II.

"I am Raven.
I have embarked on a council
to censure those who
would oppose your nature.
I discern the things of
the wild and their relation to humanity.
I reside in the region of Ucluelet,
where your once fertile reaches
are now savage and encircled
by predators. For where you were once
salty purity, you now suffer pollution.

The grey sea replied,
"Your portion is one of the stars,
and you are guided
by the constellations
named long ago by your forefathers.
Continue in the ways of the natural earth,
for you have clearly and precisely
gathered the evidence to consider
how to protect the creatures
of the sea, the air, and the land
that contains your people."

The chastening of the fields with the
harvest is as the light of the sun
and moon that sweep o'er the grain.

His body now glows in stained glass
where it was marred with wounds.

Cygnus

I.

The eleven rains came,
pattered upon the twenty-two burgundy roses
of the rose garden
and the lily-velveteen pond
where the seven swans swam 'round,
reticent and proud,
upon the morn of the mass
for the small baby sleeping
sweetly in ivory.
The rushing white birds
flew over the gates of the crystal palace.

The ashes smoldered
in the grate of his hearth,
a fire burned in the heart of royalty
as they unfolded the parchment
of the sacred tree
planted in the garden
on the day of the new prince's birth,
growing ever-onward
toward his coronation.
The first trumpet sounded, brass and beauty.
"All hail," said the peasants from the fields.

II.

Raven could not crown the shore,
so she spoke to tame it instead,
and the sea proved a domain
that was pre-eminent
as the land and sky.
She bent as the water drew back,
and picked up a rainbow-hued mussel shell.
The lucidity of the light,
pouring at that moment from the sky,
made each object of the sea
a presage to be tested.

With renown, has the sea mesmerized
with its creed of humility for generations.
A prophet of the divine,
it poured forth its oratory
of water, of the Queen of Water,
and of the creatures within it.
So I watched the young native woman
as she confronted time and nature
from the paradigm of her humanity
for she had been a prostitute on the streets
in years before.

The vineyard is heady with grapes.
A love based on true commitment
will stand the test of time, aging like fine wine.

The anointing oil flows from the broken,
and they subdue their self-pity.

Delphinus

I.

The sisterhood of enclosure—
a garden with a wall, the lime buds
of spring appearing
from the stark black apron of winter,
the gathered compassions
a christening of new life,
souls, unstained and attentive,
at the table of community
where wreaths of grape vine
foster the candles
flickering at dark.

She forgave her enemies,
growing her morals
with the maple leaf ivy
climbing the sacred white brick,
plunging her hands deep into the ground,
saying,
"The chant of plainsong beautifies
that eternal crucifix on which we have placed
our affections and the things of this world—
the purity of consciousness—
a wall upon which he is the water."

II.

The requisite surroundings
of the woods and beaches
were what gave Raven the familiarity
of a place to belong.
When I looked up from my work,
Raven was eyeing me cautiously.
She padded over in her silvery moccasins,
to where I wrote in my notebook,
and curled up at my feet.
She seemed eager to tell her story.
I listened, without judgment.

The distinction of her copper necklace,
its pendant fashioned as an obsidian arrowhead,
was made for her by one of the native
artisans in the town.
Mica had appreciated her ideologist
viewpoint, and exhibited her work
in the back of his gallery shop.
He had the resolution to view
his people who had started out poor and underfed
only to be allocated with the provision to begin again,
as distinct, defined, and unconfused.

The exhibit of life was histrionic in the hands of the elders who survived the racism, discrimination, segregation, and stigma of the real world.

One had to wear a different color of skin to
believe that cruelty could be unkind
even to the fiercely proud.

Dorado

I.

Airy and ethereal as the wind that moves
the cocoa field, patterning the chocolate beans,
pitted against her own mortality,
the woman rises to the challenge
of each new day, singing
arias in color
through the silence
of the paned glass,
slanted rite of sunlight—
a medium of rays
that once belonged to me: as gods.

When I enter a room
I take note of whose it is,
the owner of these stunning
brights and darknesses,
and to whom everything belongs,
for this person is my thesis of the hour,
and the contrasting ideas of white on white
divine, create a hundred sonnets
where the stakes are drawn
between hell and purgatory,
between heaven and the look of two people.

II.

Mica was obedient and teachable
in the ways of survival in the wood,
and he had been taught by survivalists
who had gone before him.
His disposition was one of
a cheerful temperament, rarely ruffled
by the details of life.
He had followed Raven's career
since only a few years after
she had begun making cards and prints
for the tourist shops in Tofino.

Clear, his hunting voice
would ring out over the mountains and valleys.
He called to the Great Spirit
of his people to grant
him wisdom and knowledge,
and hunted with his bow and arrow
for deer and elk.
He fished in the rivers
for salmon and rainbow trout,
and his friends stuck by him
for no one was hungry at his table.

Color can have many meanings: but the purity of love
within its bounds supersedes all.

When all that is beautiful and austere has been broken and placed in a mass grave in the earth, then the clay takes over, remakes a body into the ground, and the unsilenced voice becomes the sound of the wind or the sea upon the shore.

Draco

I.

The ocean was my stately dwelling
the wind over the navy waves of blooming brunnera,
breaking with the bridle of the shore,
blending each grain
of sand with sea salt, bitter as brine;
anonymity spoke the sails passing by,
bright and stark as white on blue,
an elderly nun bent over the dying breath of a man,
a water world of softened corners,
and the beaded necklace
of a native canoe.

A familiar shore stretched lazily in the sun,
shining in full strength on the parched cloth
of shells and tide: provings
of another time and innocence,
the resonance without regret—
a high frequency of caucus seagulls,
the lofty quality of a house of kelp,
consummate on a garden shoreline,
distinguished by the purity of horizon,
embedded with a Sistine jewel,
radiant diamond morning of virtue.

II.

Raven was captivated by the
sound of the river at dusk,
or the sea against the night sky.
She boldly struck out against
the lonely poverty of earth
for the meaning of the celestial signs
and deeper pursuit of solitude.
She knew how to quell a quarrel
and abate an argument.
She had left her old trade.
She now lived alone in a cabin near the shore.

The shore extended along
the front of the houses in both directions.
Raven walked every day, rain or shine,
and it was common to see her
pitted against the wind,
rain streaming down her face.
She was seldom
unhappy, with her artwork
and her job as a housekeeper
at the house right below the cabin
to keep her busy.

To trust again when you have been hurt,
you must make it as difficult
as possible for the person to repeat their offense.
Forgiveness is a waiting for the dark to dissipate into morn.

The church is but a babe in arms.
The young, the innocent, the forgiving—all must travel here.

Equuleus

I.

I was seventeen,
and a dozen faint vendela ivory roses
fringed the world of graduation
from childhood to feigned adult,
where the tea is steeped for a thousand years
in lofty craters of a moon,
weeping weakly through the galaxy,
a pearl earring I have never forgotten
to wear; I close my eyes,
searing the conscience of humanity
into shreds of moth-like mortality.

I sat on the edge of the patterned upholstery,
writing in a journal I could never keep,
desperate to grow up but reluctant to prosper;
my hair in tight ringlets of dependence,
and the high-backed chair of despondency,
frequented only by the stark easel
and bold paints of mind
coerced by art and its simplicity,
staggering neutrality in dissonance,
the complications of silence—
commenced rest after a note.

II.

Raven knelt in the garden,
ridding the front beds of truant weeds,
separating the marigolds around
the base of the cedars, fashioning
the blossoms of the roses
rising like spires in the arbors.
Shortly thereafter, it began to rain.
She put on the raincoat and yellow rubber boots
in the mud room, and took
the golden retriever Angora for a walk
before dinner.

When she returned,
the sun was beginning to set.
It was early September,
and the sky was already darkening
in anticipation of winter.
She withdrew from the main house,
where she had set the table and made dinner.
Looking over the garden,
she found a bunch of purple hydrangeas,
cut them for the table,
and placed them in a tall blue glass vase.

The night watchman calls upon the wall
from last sunset to first gold.
His call is a prophetic horn for the safety of a fortified city.

Call out in the night, as the watches begin.
Lift up your voices and ask for the nations.

Eridanus

I.

Children ran in and out among
the leaves of beige blooming orchids
over the pool shaped like a pinto bean.
We sat at the wooden picnic table,
Nola, with her knitting, purl
after purl, dark hair
in a braid down her back.
She gave us each a handful of dried cherries,
their soft red centers, her lenience and strength,
both the resilience and self-reliance she was known for:
with one hand, comfort, while the other stirred.

The wind blew from a new direction.
It proved that we are people probing
the heavens for rain as some look for mercy.
The waters on the stove boiled
as she cooked our soup with herbs
and brown rice, feeding multitudes
as some people break bread. Nola stood
looking out over the hillside, the wind at her back,
the North Star beginning its nightly light house gleam,
the wrinkles around her eyes, smiling and beckoning
as windows in a relic establishment.

II.

The couple who lived in the main house
were a naturopath
named Dr. Minther and his wife Nola.
They employed Raven to
keep the house,
in exchange, she lived in the cabin
up the hill overlooking the water.
There was a warm bed with a star quilt
in the wood-stove heated cabin…
she reminisced, staring out at the sea,
digging her toes into the dry sand.

I looked down and found I had been taking notes.
Now twenty-four, Raven had spent
three years in Ucluelet working
and preparing her verdict of the sea
for the First Nations People.
Her employers were knowledgeable
in the ways of natural medicine,
and had told her of a Stó:lō medicine woman
who lived near the river of the mainland.
This was whom she planned to visit in the spring.
I was intrigued.

Ancient Hill

Climb the Ancient Hill; look out over
the spiritual plains of life
and determine a future for more than
one generation at a time.

What are you waiting for? Ascend to the
high places of justice in our land.
Mediate the cause of right and speak up for the silent ones.

Fornax

I.

Sitting against a tree of bernadine bark
under the dark green shading of pines,
listening to the woodland flute
echoing over the watershed of Canadian geese,
the Métis calling from
the wood bridge over the waters,
and the voice of liberty is
a still-life in the Lodge of Broken Bark—
sketched in pencil and watercolor—
with the impressionism of future intellectuals
contrasting colors with Pau D'Arco tea.

Someone sat in the pit house
with the methodology of natural medicine;
her ideas hollered at human development,
and she was hovering over the Stó:lō exhibit.
The leather drums were worn,
the telltale resonance of musical rhythm
mixed with the quality
of natural inner beauty
rarely found with such goat-hair baskets
and hypotheses in the conclusion
of a news article about Xa:ytem Longhouse.

II.

Raven wrote a letter to
the medicine woman on the mainland
to find out what the traditions and ways were
of the people of that region, the Stó:lō.
The elderly woman had sent an invitation to
her to come visit the Xa:ytem Longhouse in the spring.
Raven had readily agreed.
Now that I knew about Raven and her plans
for March break, I anticipated
her coming right to the region
where I lived and wrote.

There was a candle burning
once again in the window
at my home in the back woods
of Bear Mountain.
I got out my notebook and began
typing away, the familiar sound
of the keyboard tap-tapping.
I had returned home from Tofino —
the sea, the salt, and the sand,
still tangled in my hair.
This time, I had hope I would get well.

Seashells lie broken and battered on the ocean floor.
How does one recover the dead, and those presumed to die?
By harvesting souls for the divine, like
the fruit of a great seashore.

The salt of the ocean repels, as a sweetness,
the disease and all pollution.

Gemini

I.

In unity we are inseparable,
indissoluble, indivisible: the cream baby's breath,
whispering a prayer for the devout.
The meter of tones and semitones,
iron and clay,
strong and regimented paired with healing.
A wreath of balsam, berries sequential,
and nature bows its burnished head
with bureaucratic respect
to institute some deeper sacrifice
than dark and the beauty of oil—then death.

I rise again.
I am a candle.
I am one million burning
before the year is through—burning in the windows,
lit because this country will not be ruled
by fluorescence.
Light a candle in the Old World
by the wailing wall,
shield it from the wind.
So they lit candles
in beeswax, soy, and paraffin.

II.

The sky was pale with morning.
A cabin stood like a wand of hyssop
just at the edge of the wood.
The logs were weathered in places
and covered with moss.
There was a table and bench
for eating outdoors, and a finely
strung fishnet for drying herbs and nettles.
The medicine woman
was collecting wild botanicals in a basket
outside the door to the garden.

I walked through the woods,
one foot in front of the other,
wondering how I had come
so unexpectedly to the Xa:ytem Longhouse,
and expecting to see Raven again.
I thought that perhaps restoring
health began with doing something
different than one had done all along.
I was hoping to find a medicine
among the First Nations that had been
passed down for generations.

Nature is a governing apologist, with
her back to the heavens.

Mother earth reigns in all free radicals
with the power of antioxidants.

Grus

I.

With all the best intentions of the florist
I measure the crimson carnations
into glass bowls for a baby shower,
coupling their colors and paring their blooms.
A new mother's smile is their humble fragrance,
as a native woman turns toward her son,
the Great Spirit turns toward us
with the falling petal of each flower,
minute by minute, a subtle reminder
that life is fleeting and precious,
as the silent moccasin disappears

Into the forest, from death we are recovered,
from sickness we are restored,
our mortal wound is given salve
of cedar and comfrey;
we are quiet warriors, walking
into the silent space,
guardians of the sacred circle, yet continue on
that we may walk healed,
if not here then in the next life.
Bring me up from the grave—
light me as a pillar of wax.

II.

When the medicine woman was finished,
she sat down at the balsam-scented outdoor table.
She took a notebook and pen out of her dress pocket,
and with a scarf, tied her shining dark hair
up once more.
She scratched on the paper. The black pen
left clean marks as she made her notes
of the pharmacopeia of the four medicines.
She did this each day.
Then she rose and retreated
back into the cabin.

I arrived at the reserve through the wood on foot,
and my presence was announced.
Raven came quickly to greet me.
"Sea!" she said, overlooking over my
long fitted crepe skirt, garments
of a florist-in-training. I had a bundle
of freesia and Queen Anne's Lace.
She smiled, and I could see
our friendship had evolved from
just an idea to an entity
of color and emotion.

The North is a woman with snowy hair and icy fingers,
waiting for summer to emerge.

The South is a flowering tropic beneath the equator, with manifold witnesses to its quartz precision.

Hercules

I.

The best of midnight poets:
under the scarlet-tinged magnolia,
the grain of the black and white lens
posed for capture—
lucid and knowing of her power,
an Armstreet cape
over her head,
the slight figure, almost breathing,
but bereft without verse
and the renascence of life
after death.

She is nocturnal,
lighting a candle,
she is an orator slowly burning,
writing a sonnet before the day is through;
a contemplation of motion
by hero—
a milky white dove
rising into the heavens,
moving a country
to action, the way lit by her
brazen beeswax and profane paraffin.

II.

Every morning, the sun crept across
the neck of wood, lighting the tansy patch,
and the wild blueberry bushes beside the log cabin.
It passed by by the potato garden,
the greenhouse of tomato plants
and the squatting shed of chickens,
though there were only two laying hens left.
The medicine woman made breakfast at the stove,
heating the hot water for blackberry leaf tea.
Naiya cooked eggs and potatoes
and sliced the tomatoes with tiny eyes.

Raven led the way through the reserve
to the log cabin of the medicine woman.
I could already smell breakfast cooking,
and observed the neat rows of wild crafted herbs
outside the door, the vegetable garden, and the wood.
It was a place where healing of the
North, South, East, and West
was not only about the medicine wheel,
but a spiritual practice of restoring the mind,
body, and soul to balance. I prepared myself
to encounter the traditions of the earth
that dated back for centuries.

Remember to walk the benign road,
of healing and reparation,
away from the virulent poisons of earth.

There is always a fragrant humble service, apart from gain,
where one benefits the lives of others.

Horologium

I.

Captivating, the delicate
paper-thin turquoise Tibetan blue poppy
resounds and the Buddhist monk echoes
down the austere hallway
in plaintive chant,
legs crossed in a lotus,
flexible and studied,
eyes closed from a far-away place,
mind like a clean chalkboard
under the rain of a sky birthed
again and again from earth to life.

I am empty when I am like the brittle bird,
soft wax melting beneath a candle,
light in my soul
which wafts in the wind
blowing to and fro through the desert lands,
bending again my skeletal hands,
nodding my anorectic mind
at the philosophy of hunger.
I take hold
of the nature of things,
ravenous and silent.

II.

With a beaded rind, the aloe plant
with its tendrils, reflected the tincture
that the homeopaths reproduce
over and over, falling like water
into a field, only a seed of an idea under miles
of sacred plants, elder bone
fragments beneath the ground,
where moccasins had been sucked into the dense
aromatic mud—
memories and artifacts
for this world and the next.

The moment I entered her cabin,
I was impressed by the immense memory
of the Stó:lō woman with dark hair named Naiya.
Her humble beginnings had taken her
to study health at some of the country's most
prestigious universities and back again.
She was gifted in both the written and oral
tradition of the First Nations and was the medicine woman
of the many Stó:lō Nation bands,
teaching several practitioners under her
in the ways of the four medicines.

Water is comforting and speaks in a thousand forms;
watering the earth is the job of all cultivation.

The evening incense burns hotly, turning our anger into the earth, then lukewarm, binding the flavors of smoke and sandalwood. When only ash is left, my sins will have dissipated on a plane where chaff is no more.

Hydra

I.

The native wild flower revels in damp soil
and partial shade. Sunshine yellow archangel;
spikes of bright flowers appear
in early spring,
and are welcomed by choirs of humming bees.
Ideal for naturalizing
with light streaming, dreaming,
drumming under trees in woodland.
Roots as it goes, deeper, deeper,
so seeps beneath the earth
almost indefinitely.

The wings of the archangel raise
the dead from beneath the earth,
where they have rested in the ground;
they take the form of sacred animals.
For is earth mortal or immortal?
Every finite thing reflects an infinite being,
like a fetus nestled in the womb
who is expelled into birth—
a new burning in the windows
lit by home hearth fires,
warm, multicolored, and flickering.

II.

The sun began to heat
the spikenard floors until they shone.
She lit a fire in the wood burning stove.
When Raven and I sat down at the table,
the medicine woman looked up with a smile.
Raven was like a daughter to her already,
although she didn't say this out loud.
She mulled it over with her conscience
because Raven had a captivating personality
and had invited me to come with her to the reserve
for the spring break to learn about the four medicines.

Of course, I would come every day
and learn what I could in such a short time,
I had agreed. Naiya was careful
to consider my medical condition,
the idea that I had cancer and whether it could
be healed to the point of remission. I had faith,
as I sat before her fire, that she knew a few things
about hope and healing that orthodox medicine
had not yet uncovered. The first thing Naiya did
was begin my detoxification process
by soaking my feet in a warm cedar bath.

The glamorous life speaks of great gifts,
and the human body speaks of Gaudi's canvas.

The gemstones of life are its virtues,
not its possessions.
The setting of holiness holds the gem of grace.

Hydrus

I. (Found poem)

India. A sapphire within the nations,
a jewel within the crown—the coffee flower
contributing to a magnificent paradise.
The climate is largely tropical
in summer, resplendent;
cool in winter, solemn and aloof.
Hence nature
has bestowed all coffee farmers with
the mystic beauty of both worlds:
enchanting, bewitching,
captivating flowering of coffee.

One can witness the elevated tall mountains,
depicting the timeless magic locked within
during coffee blossom, thousands of acres
bedecked with white flowers,
emanating a beautiful scent
with the dancing
of honeybees and butterflies.
During the blossom time—
the delicate fragrance assumes a white hue,
as the coffee flowers overpower
every other color.

II.

That morning, the two women—
one clothed in buckskin, one in a myrtle skirt,
entertained me with stories of the healing
tradition among their peoples.
Finally, Raven drew her black hair into a ponytail
and slipped out into the garden.
There the beans and corn, squash and tobacco,
ripened in the light, bright and effulgent,
turning from shadows to bright color.
The smell of whole foods cooking
rose to the loft above where she slept.

Feathers wafted to the wood floor
from the ceiling.
Cider with cinnamon was brewing on the stove.
Naiya looked out the window at the midday sun
and watched it light the wood, the meadow,
then the garden to flame.
Naiya saw in the young Raven the fearlessness
of a warrior among the First Nations People.
Her look was that of a hunter
amid the morning. Raven was
already fond of the "People of the River."

Warriors of the true nature fight the
battle within rather than without.
To win, they must relinquish all but the inmost self.

Radiant health shines down the corridor,
of darkness and disease as a ray of light.

Indus

I.

The young child's drooping head,
falling into slumber as a violet bellflower—
cherubs circle round,
the response of divinity
to innocence and youth,
sleeping in the arms of the plum tree.
Beneath the arbor,
where ivy vines climb, resinous,
the new shoot unfurls its dreamy notions,
reticent and kind,
pensive at spring in all measures.

The steady sun's warm beat,
pounding again into the soul of a child
with rapturous burning,
at the turning of each year—
agape flame—he bends in collaboration
with memory and obedience,
corresponding to unspoken heavens,
divining the boundaries of motion,
his plate of armor bold and shining,
the rainbow overhead leaving a pot of gold
for new worlds to discover under the rain.

II.

Raven looked up
at the orange sun over the Ancient Hill.
She knew that from its summit she could see
the surrounding territory for miles.
This was where the elders gathered.
It was the sacred place where
the smoke rose from their fire,
and they made treaties
with the surrounding bands.
Raven was now amid the women, however,
forbidden to climb the Ancient Hill.

Naiya sat down calmly,
and flew into the light of the sun
as an eagle; it was still early in the day
and there was plenty of time for work.
For now, she must be a bird in flight.
I contemplated, with eyes wide.
I wondered if it were possible
to wrest my soul from its confines.
The tutor of a younger generation
in the ways of botanical medicines
showed me firsthand the spiritual world.

If one waits for what is true,
a promise will be kept forever.
A broken promise is far from the
ordination of mercy.

There is a home outside the soul.
Make one's home in the deep forest,
and one's footprints will resound
energetically throughout time.

Lacerta

I.

The best statement of alkalinity
is the light blue hydrangea;
its effulgent head of blossoms
a response of the divine
to the sacrifice of gardening,
to the alkalinity of soil,
the many hours of pruning, weeding, planting,
and the benefit of seeds, unseen
germinating beneath the sky and sun
then arising in papery blossoms
that turn to vintage brown.

This house, where there is a gate
in the old stone wall around the gardens,
and we can walk for miles
unhindered, arms swinging,
boots echoing, as our cries down the valley,
seeing the countryside divulge its bloom,
pairing flowers and wild grasses alike,
waiting in their ethereal seasons
until sudden life comes forth, and they are cut,
even adorn the wreath and vase in profusion—
never failing in prolific color, baptizing the field.

II.

The eagle scanned the landscape
for a place to land, soaring with a giant
wingspan through clouds, and over
Douglas firs and pines.
Finally, she landed on a large black stone
on the Ancient Hill.
From here she looked out over the valley
to the horizon.
Within a few moments a raven
landed next to her.
They felt a soft wind ruffle their feathers.

The raven and the eagle took the privilege
of eyeing the citronella countryside
from vantage point of the transformer stone.
This gigantic rock had
been the subject of myth
since the first longhouse was
built by the river nine thousand years ago.
The original Stó:lō people
believed that the gods had
descended to earth with
supernatural powers.

If you had power to run from what would
destroy your faith, you would find
a marathon commitment.

The hope of contemplation is that revelation
will win out over information.

Leo

I.

The land was vacant and unoccupied, deserted,
the khaki broad-leaved anemone
appeared for avocation
in the garden bed,
with dry earth that cracked for want of rain;
now the master and mistress
of the old homestead
had seen spoken their elegy,
and the farmhouse moaned a dirge,
in mournful rebuttal.
Be it resolved that there is life after death.

In the grand scheme of things
do money and power suffice,
and do we lay claim to them in a desert,
practicing our songs amid the rocks,
or collect, in a meadow of wild,
the exaltation,
yet we are not senseless, trivial, or weak.
So we embark on boats to strange lands, vacuous;
the celebrity home of high repute,
a dismal force of reckoning
when falling into decay.

II.

Now the ruins of the original
Stó:lō people had been built over
with new pit houses and a longhouse;
their band was called the Lodge of Broken Bark.
A smooth and sacred rock remained,
black stone with spiritual powers,
transforming Naiya into an eagle,
high in the sky
and bringing Raven to her side
on this day of reckoning.
I could only watch and wait.

The two women were cohorts:
one elderly and one youthful with clary sage eyes,
to exhort their people
from idleness and slavery in a modern culture,
to the spiritual beings
that they were meant to become.
One an eagle, the other a raven,
they both had sharp eyes
and observant minds.
Naiya gazed at me thoughtfully.
"Your spirit is the sea," she said.

You are like none other.
Strengthen what remains.

The father of the universe calls your name,
giving you life on earth after a time of gestation.

Leo Minor

I.

As a mother separates
the cream from the milk of the fuchsia
rhododendron, collecting them in a glass jar,
the slosh of nourishment
to mortify the flesh, restraining the base
which catches at the heels of theology,
a chalky cliff, testing the sky,
as a child would write
on the pavement in summer,
"Gloria in excelsis Deo"
with a piece of colored chalk—

A bright ice
in a silver shoppe with
tiny plastic spoons,
tasting for good conscience,
old fashioned fountains
of soda water
to contrast the flat arid desert plain,
where the sun rises
out of the nivea mountain
in a gelato-blue sky
as a spokesperson to the moon.

II.

At the beginning of time,
when the Ancient Hill
had been set as
the sacred meeting place,
it was known
that the First Nations People
were to take the shapes of animals,
that the animals containing them were
to carry their spirits for their lifetime
and into eternity
in the happy hunting ground.

The raven and the eagle soared
into the blazing blue eucalyptus sky
from the transformer stone
where they had originated,
back when the earth had been
a fertile land of birth and rebirth.
The colors of red, yellow, black, white shimmered.
The medicine wheel turned round—
North, East, South, West.
"Mother Earth, come nourish
the ground of my spirit," said Naiya.

Administrate love and it will rebel.
Free love and it will heal a nation.

What are the gifts of earth and sea, of rain and
wind, of air and fire, of wood and metal except the
elements that must be brought under dominion.
The Creator threaded them in the order
of the hours, days, and seasons
like indigo marble-eyed beads.

Lepus

I.

My daughter stood beside the old oak tree
where moss grew about at random.
She turned and stared with diplomacy,
asking to take some to school,
and as the teacher requested, we complied,
prying its lecherous tendrils
from the carved bark,
formidable
as an education in tithing
the dance of nature, harvesting
our souls for the divine.

I took her by the hand,
we walked into the field
where cows roamed
and the knarled apple blossoms grew;
the shadows of suns and crescent moons
like the croissants buttered on the table,
homespun gingham tapering
the shaker table with forgiving arms.
We would never say goodbye,
we would never see
the end of immortality.

II.

Be the bear of the North, our protector.
Be the eagle of the East, our life.
Be the deer of the South, our innocence.
Be the buffalo of the West, our strength.
Let the wheel of the four medicines go 'round,
thought Raven beside her.
For we are women of great power,
and our sacred plants—
the sweet grass, the tobacco,
the cedar, the sage,
you have given us to connect us to you.

I knew I would meet the Creator of this people,
and now I had. I waded through the purple
lavender field—perhaps I would never be the same.
I mulled over the four medicines of the medicine wheel
as I walked back through the woods
to my home at the foot of Bear Mountain.
I sat on the porch after dinner
and theorized as dark descended,
the large Labrador curled up at my feet.
I sipped a steaming cup of hot
licorice tea from my favorite stoneware mug.

We are bound for a familiar shore, waves crashing
upon the conscience of time.

The broken seashell poems are scattered over the tide pools, almost neglected by years of fear and pain.

Libra

I.

Fragile in uniformity,
shaped like a willowy pewter pear
women find themselves composed of art,
of work, of decoration, of travel.
Their conscience descends down through the ages,
not the product of any one individual effort.
Fruits and flowers crown women in their glory,
and they move from one location
to another in exile and in elocution.
The milieu where woman flourishes
is the center of life.

Where the woman identity centers around her,
and where she is centered,
the arising of her life
stands alone in its power.
The changes that occur in her hands
and by her will speak of the empowerment
of a culture and its people.
For the nation trembles when
women are hurt, marginalized, or abused—
the tears of a child are never justified,
but the enduring gift of a smile.

II.

The next morning I returned.
Raven and Naiya were harvesting
the herbs growing in prolific profusion
outside the door of the log cabin.
We all went inside.
One stirred the ashes
of the wood stove into flames of smoky cedar.
The other cooked bean and rice soup
over the burner of the kitchen stove.
Several others came in for breakfast,
their dark eyes feasting after the long night.

Vials of remedies and fine oil
on the shelves against the walls
reflected Naiya's position as
a healer and woman of valor
among her native peoples.
She wildcrafted their sacred herbs,
harvested, bottled them,
and extracted their oils.
She had soothed a fever many times,
worked a salve into inflamed tissues,
healed a wound, and set a broken bone.

Many work with feverish intent to accomplish
the impossible, without joy in a natural earth.

You drew out of me a smile. Always remember,
there is a smile for every customer,
and a name for every child.

Lupus

I.

The austere constellations,
the influence of opal pearls of tapioca
in the mouth of night—
bright with sparkling moons and silken stars,
breaking dawn
in the house of the planets,
the gloss of the particular
over vague notions
of intellectual pursuits,
flipping through the glassy
stare of a magazine.

Mere chattels of reminiscence,
inciting tearful partings
with transient knick-knacks,
the symbols pealing through
movements of clear nail polish
that would propel someone to action,
evicting the skeleton from my closet,
in an old majestic house
worn over years
with contents of bureau drawers
emptied, looking for a fountain pen.

II.

That night, the twelve Stó:lō elders
donned their masks of bright paint—
red and black on carved birch wood.
The moon, the sun, the buffalo, the eagle,
the wolf, the bear, the deer, the porpoise,
the killer whale, the hummingbird, the hare,
the caribou. They sat in a circle at
the top of the hill. Each would have
a chance to speak, but first they passed
the peace pipe. A small tuft of smoke rose
from each elder behind their birch mask.

Solemn and decorated,
they circled the campfire as a dance
in the late evening then
talked into the night,
their spirits fiery with anise hues,
as guardians of their people,
the healing circle, and the talking piece.
They were the twelve word keepers
and the heritage of the oral tradition
was passed down through
the sacred choosing of the twelve.

There was a witness who kept intact the ancient tradition
of the portal of nocturnal fire.

Who sits above the stoning of the immoral,
or the burning of the witch from
a medieval village? Is there a God, or
should we be purged of all sin?

Lynx

I.

The indelible grain, small salty seeds,
pauper steel-blue stones: amaranth
communing with the ancient Aztecs,
echoing the clamor of a leafy jungle,
servile in labyrinthine maze,
diminutive guerdon, a miniscule
unassuming arbitrator—
admiring the euphonious reality
and capturing
of the endless pupil
divining the eye of humanity.

The descant was a branch,
not an extraordinary middling,
both observing and dying,
measured as contemplation
in glass cups for cooking;
a mother and father looked at each other,
studying their graces,
their differences immaterial,
the base interference
of the ordinary and ignoble,
grave, intricate, and perplexing.

II.

Eventually each elder would dance
to the center drum, perform
a ceremonial rhythm in costume
of his native band's heritage.
The sliver of camphor moon was high overhead,
illuminating the field below.
The slow chant and drum beat
echoed down the hill,
but there was no one for many miles;
it was unheard by all
but the snow owls and the milky moon.

The talking piece was given to the first,
giving him permission to speak.
"Elders," he cried out,
"we must protect our land
and our people,
for the modern world
encroaches about them
and would take them captive
to many dangerous ways and substances
that affect the mind and judgment."
The others nodded their agreement.

When womanhood is as sacred as the wind,
the spirit blows from four directions.

A child cries and must be comforted by something: if we do not hold their hand through the deep forest, society will take them away.

Lyra

I.

Hanging from the boughs—
smooth, magenta Ambrosia,
stealing through the meld of summer,
where a cardinal sang in full color.
The valley echoed back,
then waited;
when the shiny apples have ripened,
food of the gods,
they are collected in a bowl,
arranged for a pie,
slivers of concubine wealth.

Paired with no respite
under sugar and cinnamon—
sweetness imbuing the tart,
entering a woman's mind in the marathon for survival,
with the steady gaze of a withered
old apple tree, looking into the apple of your eye
until it fades into the dark.
We cannot but fashion
in our wrinkled hands,
a truer core, a milky white fruit,
and the peel falls to the ground.

II.

The second elder spoke,
"We must not pray for strength," he said,
"but for guidance and direction."
He passed the talking piece.
The third elder spoke,
"The two powers at war within us are
the desire for power and the search for life."
The fourth elder spoke,
"We must have a smudging ceremony
in the longhouse next week
to create solidarity in the medicine wheel."

We sat below the Ancient Hill.
and the fire in the night
left wisps of melissa smoke over the field.
Naiya, Raven, and I were three women
who knew the four medicines could heal a tribe,
bringing them into balance, wisdom, and purity.
There was a future that would bring light
to the eyes of many after us,
decades and centuries of freedom,
unlike the lighting of a candle
and then the light of a nation.

There is a doorway to nations
to pass through; virtue is placed on our heads like a crown.

The soul declares that a rainbow of light
will be issued from its prism.

Mensa

I.

In a flurry of voices, the clamor
became a tumult at the handful of marine fish,
the bountiful salty throng,
fiery under the torrid elements
cast a complexion of hand shadows,
rejection calling from bruised disadvantage,
bearing the cursory famine,
waiting in a covetous barrenness,
reaching to receive a nobility's indulgence,
under the lament of a small boy's prayer
and generous divinity.

The five thousand: husbandry in embrace,
duality of freedom and oppression,
harnessing and roaming
with baskets of bread
over the vast array of peoples
afflicted by marred stares,
the divorce of the starved and overfed.
One was a sepia bird pecking at the dust,
one discarded manna.
The person by person communion
left a gift of exhortation.

II.

When I returned home,
Wen was sitting in a chair on the porch.
He looked up at me with his jaunting chin
and questioning florid eyes.
"Sea, the minstrel would like to bring
you some rosehip oil. She is worried for your health.
Is there a way that we could come out for a visit?"
Wen, the true and living saint of the modern world
knew more than I did about rekindling life
and lighting a fire of restoration and grace.
He had relit the candles of many burned-out souls.

I knew somehow,
if this pathway through the woods
to a Stó:lō medicine woman's log cabin
was part of my journey,
he would make it with me;
I knew he was unafraid.
"Wen," I took his hand,
"trust me on this one…
the four medicines here are deeper than I know.
I need the balance of the longhouse and the natural earth,
and, I think they also need you."

Those who are athletes practice daily to live,
compete to win, and run to endure.

I hover around the skirts of my mother,
and she is the healer of nations—
not just mine alone, but that of each
language, dialect, and people group.

Microscopium

I.

My head bent at the bright light,
the mauve clock vine,
steady on the brick,
staying its simple prelude to morning,
ripening valor as parchment leaves
scripting an old song
from the ancient path
through the wilderness,
for a word with a nun in a garden—
and for the benefit of the deaf, the blind, the mute,
before death would take us in with open arms.

I rise unseen, a spiritual invasion, stealth
beneath the rays of morning;
as Hatzic lake unfurling its piney arms
to the hills and the skies.
Window of the articulate future,
ruling all nature with its child-like breath,
fiery heart, and contemplative whisper.
Let silence rule your speech,
walk into the quiet place of unspoken love.
The valleys erupted into spiels
of purple, green, and black.

II.

The minstrel awoke.
She had been sleeping under the boughs of a tree.
Her harp and flute were carefully tucked into her bag,
from her walk of many miles the day before.
The morning bubbled like a jasmine brook,
the minerals of a spring eddying downstream.
The water was a cool emollient,
and as she gathered some water to drink,
she began to sing.
"Lulala, lulalei, the kindness of God is compassion,
and he will lead us on his way."

She shielded her eyes,
and looked into the distance
toward the city of Vancouver,
towering like an etched soapstone.
She could barely remember the journey
she had taken the day before,
following the clay road toward the city.
It was still early as she left again
on foot toward her destination.
The prominence of roofs as she
approached the dormant city slated the horizon.

Once in a lifetime we come to our senses.
We ask for more than what we deserve.

The heavens have placed the Catholic
church and the First Nations People
side by side. And to what end? Surely we
will find a reason to this enigma,
a solution to this complicated riddle.

Monoceros

I.

Independence did not speak of our frailty,
pioneering a reservoir of sable persimmons,
the kitchen, curtained in a customary nod
to plates, saucers, and silverware,
the inestimable conversation a lull
to the hot and humid California afternoon,
from the infamous blue eggs
to the long wood table,
servings for each invited guest
of sun-iced tea, fresh milk, and green tomatoes.

Her lenient grace,
that of my grandmother
with six robust children,
settling her household at dusk,
writing letters with sealed envelopes,
greetings in ink were felicitous—
her dark red hair and creamy skin
an adage to the hard-working,
and her grandchildren noted the pomp
of Seignac, occupation of the oil painting
A House of Cards.

II.

The minstrel knew that there was
a company of prophets in the city,
that they might give her a revelation
that would guide her in where she was to go.
She walked and sang the rudimentary notes of a chant,
the footprints from her boots
left an imprint behind her on the road.
She sang, and the song was a dirge,
unlike a funeral procession under the
morbid insults of men. The tune was even
and compelling, and they glanced her way.

As the minstrel came to the heart of the city,
it was late afternoon.
She came to the great door of a cathedral, and stopped.
Ledum oil wafted from under the frame.
Would the rector be able to speak with her?
The rector was about to leave for the day,
but he opened his office door and invited her in.
He gave her a cup of water, for she was thirsty.
"Here is what we know—Certainty, that
what began yesterday will remain today.
Tell me your story," he requested.

The contrast of light against darkness allows
for the light of one small candle,
burning in the night.

She was dressed in black velvet, and the
stars were her diamond necklace.
This is what I knew of the Empress Clay—
she was the nightlife of the Western world.

Musca

I.

What I believe, is the harvest of
the coral narcissus flower,
the gift of one daffodil per village,
or the ode of a boy
who drank from a stream in a wood,
the nectar of self
poured out into black bowls
of oily petals.
What cost me everything
was my wandering heart, winsome
to other people's Buddhas.

On finely arched altars
of white marble,
the fruits, grains, and flowers
spilled from copious plates.
Before the night is over,
I will
have refused to bow
in reminiscence of an earlier day,
when I thought you
were everyone and everything,
and I would never worship an idol.

II.

The light came streaming down.
It lit the minstrel's head, in hushed solace.
She paused.
"I grew up in the cathedral close.
The nave was my home as much as the seaside,
the windy road, and the garden of galbanum.
While my mother stoked the fire of our cottage,
my father was the caretaker of the church
and kept the place of worship
in immaculate order.
I was taught to create music from an early age.

"The harp and the pipe organ
were not foreign to me, and
so I learned to play the piano,
the flute, and the guitar.
I went to school and trained
as a lyricist in our small town in Europe.
I was taught by the masters to play Bach,
Handel, and Mendelssohn.
Hours I spent
in composition benefited the church,
for I played often for the early service."

To become more normal is never the reason we live.
The incongruities of life create its tapestry of colors.

We live for freedom from the religion that sent
us to a place we could not withstand,
for a reason we could not understand.

Norma

I.

All in one bowl,
the sunrise oranges glow hotly,
acrid with vengeance,
vowing their resurgence
in retribution,
waiting in anarchy,
resisting mediocrity,
as the juicer whirs away
paring their juicy hearts to pieces
right before breakfast,
they folded their hands to pray.

The continued perpetuity
was on the blessing,
surrounding and keeping safety
at the center of mankind's ills,
seeking not the downfall of another,
but his peace and
that he would bring peace to others.
His dialog would be
an investment in the future
and its truce with dogma.
So was founded a capital of peacemakers.

II.

"How remarkable," said the rector,
listening to the minstrel's story.
"Please continue."
"My mother died when I was sixteen,"
said the minstrel, "leaving my father
with two children, myself and my sister,
an apprentice of the stained glass window.
I still composed in my usual way,
the lilting tones of my harp predicting the melody,
yet I knew there was something more for me to do in life.
I anointed my neck with patchouli oil
and waited for a call from God.

"When I thought I had heard his urgings,
whispering to depart, I left in the night
to travel the open road across Europe."
"What fascinating adventures you have had," said the rector.
"But you shall tell me more tomorrow,
for it is getting late.
Come, stay tonight at the manse with me and my wife."
The minstrel agreed, for she was tired from her long journey.
They departed from the cathedral
and went to have a quiet supper
under the eaves of the nearby manse.

The rushing air of the open road has a refrain of repetition,
a liberation into consciousness, as a whale
rises from the deep springs
or a young child breaks a ribbon of contest.

Every covenant people group will receive a call in the night. Urgent is the whisper: rise and respond—and not to no avail.

Octans

I.

I had a cat named Amiel once—
she was sunset-sweet and ate nibs
with a white bib,
the silver service was brought in
twice per day,
with chocolate cake and frosting,
dusted with white lace sugar.
So we set the table
with her golden spoons,
poured her a cup of creamy goat's milk,
and she grew a glossy coat.

"Why is your house made of silver and gold?"—
I called into the night,
and the Siamese-Persian came in,
sitting on her warm rug before the fire;
she had hunted the mouse before day's end,
she had traversed at the bridge over the lily pond,
she was a thing of beauty,
companion to the dark woman
of many colored flowers,
placing them with cut and bathed stems
in a bamboo bowl.

II.

After the minstrel had retired for the night,
the rector still sat at the dining room table.
He was intrigued that she had arrived at just this time,
and flipped through his Bible.
His wife was at the counter, chopping fennel.
"What do you think of this young woman
who has traveled so far,
with only the urgings of God as direction?"
"I can only think of the passage in 2 Kings," he responded,
"'Call a minstrel, and she will play for us.'"
"Very well," his wife replied. "She will play for us."

On the porch, Wen and I had come to a consensus.
"In three days from now, Raven will be returning
to her home in Ucluelet," I said to Wen.
"We will have a smudging ceremony in the longhouse."
"Will the minstrel come and play," I invited,
"as a way of uniting the balance
between the way of 'The Gregorian Minstrel',
and the drum beat of the Stó:lō tribe?"
Wen's eyes scanned the mountains of Mission
on the horizon, and his approval
resounded as a human heartbeat.

The Angel Song

Arioso of Virtue

Virtue has honesty as its trademark,
and loveliness as its hallmark.

We are bound by the serums of the masters, their
plays upon words, their songs, their voices.

Ophiucus

I.

The kindness of gold on white,
the polish of its reclaim,
the stream from which it flows
within the mind,
the mountain from which it is mined,
when all within us is hounded
for a virtue, of the hero's
worth delivered, his noble speech—
the precipitate of such smooth worth
opposing all malice,
against cruelty as cowardice,
the cross forever in its setting of zircon-like valor
and nature's coincidental applause;
the pause with all silence,
the final wave from solitude.

II.

The next day, the minstrel
was led into the sanctuary of the cathedral.
Granted, she could play the pipe organ,
the grand piano, the flute or harp,
but she chose instead to begin
the morning with a simple prayer
to the divine nature for assistance,
then she strummed her piece on the guitar.
The rector was pleased that
she was so gifted, and hummed
to himself as he went about his work.

At last, the rector called the minstrel
into this office. He had decided the church
needed a director of music, and was willing to
pay her a monthly salary to stay
there at the cathedral for three and a half years.
She would live downstairs, burn the helisynchrum
incense, and play throughout the day.
The minstrel conceded that this humble
beginning was an occupation
she most desired. She was willing to
stay on for three and a half years, she replied.

Where you build your house, therein your heart will dwell.
A soul must be enameled with compassion
and fortified with love.

Striking a chord of passion, we set out as youth.
But it is maturity which grounds us,
directing the journey of life.

Orion

I.

The purity of silver on white,
an attentive pursuit of contrast,
the polished spoon at each place setting,
and ray of each firmament cloud,
the house no gore will pierce
in its heroine of the hour, poet
of the meek and modest, lowly;
no superfluous gesture of the wealthy
is a blow to stealth of the midnight thief—
the hysterical notion of the candlestick's demise
casting tarnish at each step,
the shadows of its slander
no decoration of virtue
and nature's boisterous clamor
is now a silent moment.

II.

I sat looking out over the garden,
and my child Rain colored
the pages of her coloring book
with thin purple and white crayons.
I watched the lentil soup on the stove
out of the corner of my eye,
while knitting a tri-colored scarf.
The three hues of the yarn
represented three nations of my country
that I knit together unreservedly:
the French, the English, and the First Nations.

The rain fell outside and watered the rock garden
of juniper, and my mind played with the essentials
of what composed unity without compromise.
Here is where I thought of the resolution
of conflict being in the essence of collaboration.
The onus for each nation to,
in autonomy, rise up and come together
for the purpose of a healed people group.
I thought of Raven and her treatise of the sea.
She knew that the natures of wild and savage,
contrasted with civilized and sane, and were interdependent.

My tongue was a glowing coal. My coat was of hot embers.
My hair was dark as olives and my skin, clear as snow,
when I became an apprentice of the stained glass window.

I was an artist without an art.
Many will now hear my voice where it has been silenced.

Pavo

I.

The chivalry of bronze on white
rising to salvation
in humility, the sword upon a stage,
and the earth a cycle of gestation,
with spring rising from where winter meets its death—
the heroine blossoms—painted as the lips of a tree
speaking virtue to the sky and streets,
gesturing without apathy in articulated
splendor, capturing summer's brave end
as the light fades its branches,
opposing its brightness,
reddening its leaves
and applauding the gloss as they fall,
pausing just before the ground—
autumn's farewell before repose.

II.

I had finished writing my volume of
poetry, *The Rite of Spring* and had sent it to
my publisher. Somewhere in the embers of the fire
was a life deeper than words
that I wanted to capture right at this moment
when life and death hung in the balance.
At the same time, the minstrel would
be in the middle of a Song Without Words on the piano.
I was growing bright-eyed at what I
cherished most in this world,
and although I had had to spend more time healing
than I relished, I imagined myself the wildness of the shore.

I had much in common with the three women.
Somehow, eating oregano out of the garden,
lighting the candle in the wreath of spruce,
and knowing grace was bringing healing
to my body and soul like an exercise that had to do
with letting go. I realized at some point
before the last three days were over,
that from the first Naiya had been
more interested in whether
I was ready to die, than if I knew
about living with my hands tied behind my back.

Kinship was always wasted by criticism. Saints spent their time fortifying the minds of people with words that were deeply meaningful.

The ashes of our incense in the cathedral
close were buried in a secret location,
or sprinkled over the garden of roses
and thorns of the incarnadine.

Pegasus

I.

The vintage dignity of copper on white,
I was in a melancholic mood
and forgot to visit Color My World
before I painted the wall,
a rising gray barrier
between east and west,
the graphite on a page;
no altruistic response
to the festering shame
of negligence,
the disparity of governments,
my despondent constitution
concluded with the wall
in pieces
and a diagnosis for liberty.

II.

Naiya sent me home
to my child Rain with an armful of sage
for the burning and onychra oil.
The sky was thundering
before a downpour, and I ducked
under the doorframe,
hearing the fluttering of wings.
As I searched for its source,
I saw a sparrow had found its way
onto the porch, and was trapped
under the eaves.

I quickly called for Rain to come and watch
the sparrow, and with a towel,
captured the small creature
then released it back into the air.
It flew up and over the well,
returning to the trees and its nest.
I pondered this gregarious sign
of nature, not yet predicting
that the outcome of the sparrow
was one for any ill person returning
to their true home in the heavens.

She once had a garden of flowers far
off in the woodland meadow;
for as the myth of the wildflower goes,
the sunset with its fading rays
puts its head in her lap.

A creator of verse is harvester and gatherer:
lovely but frightened of their own power,
reclusive if at all possible.
Their elements are the melding of
both imagery and wisdom,
a gold and silver entwining.

Perseus

I.

The fortitude of iron on white,
a loamy intimation,
voices to introduce the empire
which rises steadfast and immortal
out of an ocean of constellations,
a proverbial shore of sea stars
from the cadence of bladderwrack;
mitigating against stoicism,
dancing on waves of brine,
thirsty in the wake of control—
the almost corpse escapes
without aperture,
in a clamor of windchime songs.
Then silence…the quiet lingers,
the mansions are filled with the dead.

II.

I watched the constellations that night
from the log cabin—with Raven
and Naiya, as the medicine woman
stoked the embers of her nuanced fire.
We knew, on the Ancient Hill,
the elders were meeting once again.
There was a long moment between us.
Somehow the very life of the people
depended on the chant. The drum beats
sounded in the distance, reverberated
over the cultivated geraniums and wild grass meadows.

The elders had spoken together to enlist
the four medicines of the medicine wheel
before, but now they also knew that
the preparation of whole foods and wild game,
shedding the old cloak of alcoholism
and drug addiction, went back to the ancient roots
of their people, went before
the ways of the white man—
to a simple invisible footstep on the forest floor,
an unmarked, unscarred youth,
and a nurtured, not coerced childhood.

When life can only be found in bureaucratizing
power, it is time to get creative—
dance, paint, design, decorate, color, and
write until you see an eternal life—
a mathematical pattern which repeats itself.

To be without worry, anxiety, or pain, you alone have the key.
Unlock the door.
Only you know the end goal of leaving
everything in your old life
to live what you believe.

Phoenix

I.

The delicate healing of clay on white,
its traversing through the divine iris, kinetic
from messianic earth,
laced throughout the cosmos,
deep within the ground:
the teacher smeared clay over
a blind man's eye,
nobility over poverty in a gesture
of compassion to capture
the very essence of miracle and its opponent death.
Hell pitted its cowardice against virtue,
the life from which it came,
the murmurings of a crowd
gave pause in the soaring heat,
rising into the atmosphere.

II.

The minstrel left the sanctuary
for her bed downstairs in the close
where she slept, the bergamot music
of the pipe organ still echoing in her soul.
She had played a Bach Prelude and Fugue
that afternoon, and its solemn precision
had a calculated guess at maximum capacity,
for guests had wandered in from the street
listening to the mighty chorale,
wept in their untoward pain, and not remiss,
dabbed at their eyes with handkerchiefs.

The minstrel would direct the choir and singing
the next day for communion, then head out with Wen
for the open countryside of Mission
and the longhouse ceremony.
She was looking forward to the opportunity
in this journey of her soul,
which someone had once deemed clarity,
in which she would tie herself to the church
unlike the monastic of old, with a vow of poverty
and enclosure. Wen was a man of character,
wearing the quiet generosity of Saint Wenceslas.

There was a healing moment when a master created.
There was a pause while he rested.
The virtuoso sings during the week and then reposes
in a Song Without Words.

You may dwell under a nation of unwilling people,
until they have heard what you have to say.
It was those virtues that embedded
themselves in my soul like gemstones.

Pictor

I.

Demure fashioning of love from red petals,
smooth, resinous,
the colors of effulgent cloth and heels,
handbags, and scarves,
bold designs and glittering metals.
The captive embrace of the red carpet,
the bright lights of beauty,
the bitter nostalgia of yesterday,
and glowing hot flames of fashion
tied with the knots of perfume,
regal heads, queens of the Sahara,
yoked beyond the caliber
of news reporters and paparazzi,
like lions and giraffes far off in the sand
drinking at water holes in the midst of desert.

II.

When the minstrel and Wen
had started their ministry to the community of
the Downtown Eastside, the addicted and hungry,
the poor and lonely, they had scarcely dreamed
they would tread the snow and see it
melt in the hearts of men,
and three cistus miracles of
Christ's sainthood would appear to them.
For one, the minstrel appeared
and disappeared at one time on the road, arriving
in another inconspicuous location unannounced.

A second sign, she was mixing both cinnamon
and sugar for the rector's wife
when the mixture turned to curry
before she could taste it.
A third miracle, she healed the bones of an elderly
woman who had had osteoporosis for eight years.
The minstrel during her time at the cathedral
wrote over one hundred songs, to the music
of the harp, guitar, and organ.
She was a prolific songstress and readily
composed impromptu for her audience.

I copied down the words twelve times in calligraphy
and gave it to the children of the cathedral
close to sing before bed:
The Huron Carol.

All your saints would stand beside you one day in empathy, painstakingly brought to life until their icon eyes sparkled with light and fire.

Pisces

I.

The sacred orange of generosity,
surreptitious and homespun fruit bowl—
wooden in the light of afternoon—
apples, bananas, plums, and nectarines,
painted in oils of benevolence
on my canvas.
The even, circular lines of hope
amid the poverty of hunger
blur the boundaries of the white empty page.
A mirror of measured lenity,
clemency of pity,
is the hand of the painter
at the summit of noonday.
Mildness of blessing, chasing round
and round in agreeable merit.

II.

I took up oil painting
in the same room with Rain
before Raven had come out.
Now, we both had an easel and
created a still-life of sorts
on canvas. It was a gift
for Raven, to say farewell.
I would take them to
the longhouse that night.
I painted an arbor of roses,
Rain painted the fruit bowl.

After almost an hour,
our concentration waned,
so I put Stravinsky's *The Rite of Spring*
on the stereo, and Rain
wandered out to play.
I harvested the lemon balm in the garden
beside her. For a seven year old, I thought,
she was innocuous with a toothy smile
and her grandmother's good looks.
I had tried to get her to wear dresses growing up,
but she was a tomboy at heart.

Your true character would appear,
it was the one moment where you
said no to victimization
and yes to martyrdom. For this be a strange calling,
to purposely relinquish being poor and weak.

I stood for many hours before my artistry of stained glass. I was not alone in the anticipation of a glorious result. My father stood at a distance.

Pisces Austrinus

I.

The yellow tolerance of lemons
growing in the raw Californian heat;
sheltered in the branches,
accepting and informing the sunlight
to stay and ripen
what once was young
into a wrinkled smile.
Dot dot Botticelli—the artwork of the masters
are the lemon half-moons
glowing and drowning in my glass,
tart and spring water-fresh:
my mouth is a canvas
of tastes and textures,
my whipped meringue
is the steady hand of white acrylic.

II.

As for myself, I had always dressed in
vintage style.
My clothes were often linen,
and I had grown up with the scent of clove pomanders.
Rain, on the other hand, dressed however
she felt best—her father had gone to Japan,
humbly walked in the rice fields,
and decorated not his soul
with false pretenses. We usually
waited for his return, without criticism,
he hated to be criticized.

My love of long skirts,
wool coats, and leather boots
all called themselves to form
as I dressed for the ceremony
at the longhouse. I thought
over the past two weeks,
again in contemplation,
at how to thank Raven
for her connection to the healing
of the medicine woman,
and my reunited sense of God.

I tolerate what I cannot change; I deeply
value love when it takes root.
I can now see what it was made of, by what kind of tree it is.

The silence over the water was broken
only by the paddles of a canoe.
When someone has travelled for many
miles to reach their homeland,
they are the recipients of grace.

Puppis

I.

A green-eyed patience stares at
the almost-winter hazelnut trees,
the reticent tap beneath the spring;
today comes swiftly as the wind,
yesterday parts as the autumn-parched leaves,
tomorrow will fulfillment bring,
a chance tryst beneath the sister pines,
where mother moon shines merrily
through the drought of clouds,
too long without the linen rain—
flying, a low angel over the fields.
The shadow world shifts
its black and white ellipsis
into beaded wild grasses, burrs
in the change of time and blackberry blossoms.

II.

Wen and the minstrel arrived
at my doorstep around suppertime.
I had anticipated them
looking as healthy and robust
as two children of God could be,
and their faces glowed with myrrh.
There was to be a full moon that night.
We sat at the shaker table,
held hands for grace along with Rain,
ate chili and cornbread by candlelight.
Then it was off to bed for Rain.

This was an anticipated time.
We began the walk to the reserve
with a flashlight beaming ahead.
We talked animatedly as we strode
through the wood: Was it not God
who healed in every area of our lives?
Did we not pray with fervor,
then turn our heads at the miracle
in front of us on a daily basis?
Were we not to be used for his purposes
this very night, to mend, and to heal hearts?

Nuanced as a shade of desert in
the morn, or eye of the raging storm,
the woven shawl in deep hues of midnight,
the blueberries on a token branch, bright.
The indigo began, seeped the sky into
the iris of the young, like sea.

I reached into the new light from the dark;
with arrows from my quiver, struck my mark.
The stars fell from the sky into my pouch.
Red salmon berries, I tasted with my mouth.
I pounded leather skins to smooth remorse,
and roasted meat by fire which prayer endorsed.

Pyxis

I.

The joy of blue glass,
the vase, the bowl,
tinted and shaded as the sky,
with sister stars, the anise
and cardamom pods,
in constellations of pungent sweetness.
Tomato seeds,
ready to grow
in the dialect of soil,
and the potter's directives
a warm hum of life-giving words
enameled over the silence
of neglect and starvation.
A pail of well water,
transparent and authentic.

II.

We walked in single file.
The minstrel had shouldered her stringed
harp for the journey to the Lodge of Broken Bark.
I came behind her, and Wen finished the line,
with a bundle of spearmint, humming to himself.
We were three kings of the Orient,
bearing gifts of royalty now
for the Christ child,
only this tiny babe's beauty
was robed in rabbit skin
and rested under the angel song.

My thoughts concerning my
healing journey of the last two weeks
were reticent, whereas Wen
was more outspoken.
The minstrel sang as she walked.
"What do you intend to play?"
I asked.
"You'll see. This is a prophetic night.
We come bearing gifts,"
she said. "Not just our own
but the gifts of the nations."

I am thankful for each living thing here:
the wood is my home and that of the deer.

We sit by quiet streams and paint the sky.
It is the colors of the indigo, by and by,
that reminisce of older days—the elders laugh,
to find that we are still a peopled path.

Reticulum

I.

The goodness of a purple crinoline
as a ballet measure, to the barre with graceful limbs,
ready to debate the radiance, as a dark fruit
takes in the sun, sanguine as a dancer in leotard:
an equitable fit for a mysterious woman
with a vivacious postmodern congruity
as her mandate, seeking a revered vision,
a courage angel standing, arms out, insensible—
the bluntness a prohibition, and aureole
refusing the dross with eagle-eyes.
She is desirous, faintly yearning, learning to dance.
What permanence she dreaded
became the equanimity of composure.
Singing as we are sung to, loving as we are being loved,
with each abating faculty, unfettered.

II.

"Your mothering of Rain
and your Sea nature are unequivocal,"
Wen was emphatic.
"The Stó:lō people will love your fitting in
with their enigmatic spirit world.
They dance around a glowing fire
and the burdensome issues dissipate like fine peppermint oil.
Are we now just beginning to talk,
as a child would who has come of age,
to discern his own needs,
and care for others with sagesse?"

"Before, it seems to me,
we were like baby birds,
but now, we fly,
descend on the parched field
of communication. And I'm shocked.
You were always so precise and orderly
at saying no.
Now you must say yes, to something
you have no knowledge of,
gaining only by intuition
and relationship," Wen surmised.

Where rain turns itself out of the sky,
there is a spring in the heavens,
continually pouring, and I place my water
barrel on earth to match the witness
that the water is here.

I would not be rained out by the bad weather,
but would continue to speak into the distance
of a life with water…
blue as a blue room, or a pen's ink on a page,
squaring words to joy, reaping heaven's boy.

Sagitta

I.

The practicality of the brown shoes,
selected carefully behind the glass store window.
Every fall smelled like new shoe leather,
gripped the sidewalk, walked to school.
New paper, lined notebooks,
pencils all with sharp points preceded
texts to be read, and handwriting lessons
on the green chalkboard.
Noting that the creative authors
were in a small library
in the corner of the room,
I, when standing in the book nook,
could thumb through
Mere Christianity along with
Bridge To Terabithia.

II.

"If healing is about relationship
rather than method or principle,
then I too am a bird.
I'll fly when my wind of inspiration
comes to me, I'll even fly in desperation,
in hunger, or in joy.
I'll fly," said the minstrel.
Her long blond hair was separated
into a hundred tiny braids. She smiled, at ease.
"I think we'll anoint you with holy basil tonight, Sea."
This was an old and mutual friendship, she was wise.

When we reached the longhouse,
the full moon had come out for the rite of spring.
We entered a Lodge of Broken Bark
where the Stó:lō people
had already found their places seated in a circle.
The twelve elders sat at the top of the lodge,
with Naiya and Raven as the guests of honor.
We greeted them as old friends,
they invited us in to sit beside them.
The native drummers circled round, with a rhythm
stark as a whale's breath into the open.

I am the muse of dawn and arid magenta flower.
The sun rises, a son—and moon, a daughter.
I am the sting of the bee, and the warm perfume of nectar.
The breeze is stolen like a kiss in the heart of laughter.

The maid of yesteryear stands frozen in time,
and the calendar of seasons receives its pencil-mark,
hills are drifting with the seed of cottonwood, mine.

Sagittarius

I.

The self-control of black velvet,
centered as a choir
with the accompaniment of strings,
the hollowed mouths, surrounding the note
like small pools of wax. Then rest.
She walked and sang, and the footprints
from her leather boots left an imprint behind her.
The song was threnody,
bittersweet watch over the night:
like a nightingale's tone,
hung over the branches
and the vestiges of time.
She sat beside the monastery wall
at Westminster Abbey, and composed in her usual way,
refusing to war with moths for the light.

II.

The table at the back of the longhouse
was piled high with food,
the music of the natives, their chant
and melody was intrinsic
with the smudging, the pungent smoke,
and the four medicines.
Unlike the triage of burning sage, cedar, and sweet grass,
there was a cleansing aroma
that burned deep within
the lungs. We all breathed
deeply of Wen's cypress oil.

It was a traditional Stó:lō smudging ceremony,
with the entire reserve present.
After Naiya had a chance to speak,
she extended the podium of her knowledge
to Raven, who then extended it to me.
We had become longtime friends,
and knew these last moments of
the healing circle created in our sharing
would last forever in our memories
in this Lodge of Broken Bark,
named for the Huron Carol.

I am the mother of all nature and all peoples,
dark, light, and beautiful in the valleys, under the trees.
They stand through the years, waiting for ease of sustenance,
but this country only permits hard work.

Now I see them, standing in line—asking for food,
they are given free bread.
Now I ask them, do they want to dine under the stars,
be walkers of the forest?

Scorpius

I.

The white dove of peace
polished on my shield,
I shall go forth,
my face set chaste, noble, redeemed.
As the light brightens from dawn to noon
each day, so enlightenment
begins, grows, on journey's familiar wearing,
and the sky pares away from the road ahead.
The prominence of roofs
and the Châtelet des Tourelles fortify the horizon,
as I approach Orleans.
My banner raised before me,
I lift the siege, of unspoken words,
of silence, and of hunger—
by my army of poets.

II.

A healing circle:
we had been outside of relationship
and received an invitation
to come in.
We entered, innocent
and asking.
Our wisdom had all
but disappeared,
and we had renounced our fear
and found our deepest dream—
the singer, and the song of ylang ylang oil.

When healing comes in
reunion with others,
in the community of fellowship,
there is a partaking of nourishment
like the soup of maize, beans, and squash
that gives thanks for each day we live,
and even the moments we die.
For we die to the old life,
the ways that would destroy us,
and take up our staff of
human life as intimately precious.

Ahead, far into the distance, I shout:
make way for your children—
they sit at your feet, they will understand…

Because your myth will change them from fearful to true.

Sculptor

I.

The clear purpose of artistry,
forward in reticence, never tired
or subjugated; what nervy letters you sent,
on the tails of the greats
with chisels and marble busts,
shavings of punctuality falling to the ground.
You collect your alms in a gourd,
the light comes streaming down—
it foreshadows the head of the Catholic church
in its hushed solace at drawing night.
There is a particular time
when the poverty of earth will eclipse the royalty of heaven.
It is that time, the nutmeg leaves,
highlighted through the surrounding branches,
waft the oil perfume of sainthood.

II.

There was the smallest unit of the bone-building cell,
and the bones of the native people's
ancestors, imminently sacred,
buried beneath the longhouse, then there was
the symbol of character,
a person's integrity within their bones.
All came into focus when I had cancer,
as I, suddenly as the outpouring of petit grain oil,
saw Wen begin to speak.
Then I knew that he saw his God
and the Great Spirit as one and the same.

Wen found no barricade
between himself, his wealth,
and the poverty of the People
of the River, or their affliction,
for on the Ancient Hill
was a place where they met with the Creator,
he recreated them from the inside out.
Their people had extended to him
a deep resonance
and the aroma of altruism
to beset his sterling honesty.

The lighter shades of kindness and truth,
the darker shades of forgiveness and reparation—

I create a portrait of a new nation,
where people are recreated by their own joy,
buffered by their solitary creed.

Scutum

I.

The grace of pink glow across the sky,
she shouldered her harp as an ambassador,
and followed the road into the distance.
Pleasant ode, plucking the metal strings,
the sign appeared before her,
a prophet's symbol, rhapsody,
no longer imprisoned by the missive,
but a pardon at her disposal.
The minstrel had traced the minute proceedings,
as a singer memorizes the ballad
or a troubadour fashions a melodic
compound: the bantam denouement
echoed down an old cobblestone street
in Gastown, where the steam clock
was a prodigy of science and ingenuity.

II.

"I am the sea. I cannot die. I give life
to all the people of the earth.
I spoke to you of when the world was young.
I inspired the mind of humanity
to care for the natural earth and its inhabitants.
I walked with you and your vial of
frankincense along the road
of restoration, to the place of reparation of wrongs.
Now I call you out to form an allegiance
that would start with the lighting of just one candle—
to reunite our country with the sacred,
to bring unity of thought, purpose, and direction.

"When we are one, we are one million burning.
When we can afford to do
what is best for our children,
they will thrive and be cared for.
There are so many short-cuts,
so much these days that is about
what is quick and easy, but I call you to more.
We must educate others as to
what is humane and ethical,
to the four medicines, to their virtues,
balancing to the soul and mind."

I am softened over the years,
by a spiritual awakening that quickens the mind,
and subjects the soul to a real world beyond reckoning.

Where, in the depth of night—
the stars awake and alive—
is the man of Canada, the woman of our nation?

Serpents

I.

O the thankful peach soul of a rose,
baiting summer with its nectar,
pressing petals in the folds of books
until they dry and crack with fragility,
a subtle perfume wafting
from the pages, potpourri,
mixed in the abode of literature.

My hybrid tea grew
at just the moment
when the sun was about to set,
from morning to evening
was the glory of childhood Victorian dusk.
London Drugs, in British accent,
with a cup of Yorkshire tea.

The cream was poured,
the china teapot was hot for guests
who happened by,
looking for a bite of McVities,
in chocolate or oatmeal—
a taste of this biscuit or that
in plainsong—
all blossoming like roses
beside the Métis, Inuit, and First Nations,
the renegade thorn, hidden behind our backs.

II.

In stellar progression, the midnight air
had spun its course, stars, unlike a coarse basket
woven of goat hair, dyed with mahogany stripes
of the dreams of sea and solitude.
The constellations had breathed
their gifts of direction and wisdom to man,
of virtues imbedded like the tourmaline
and champagne diamond,
oil of cassia from tightly woven
bottles, the bright crimson and jade beadwork
of the tribal women, passed down in tradition.

The purse of the Stó:lō people was
filled with the measure of wealth
that only once per galaxy gingerly touches earth.
The elders motioned to the minstrel,
she came forward,
procured her harp,
and gently strumming,
began her prophetic song.
She had thought of this long ago,
when she had visited the company of prophets.
So she sang her gift to the First Nations People.

Children of the
Forest Free

Where are the people with the wound that
earth created, without love to heal?

Life is but a reflection of the people of its heart—
they look in the mirror and see success instead of failure
when I am the spirit of the next generation.

Earth's Garden and Crowns
of the Nations

The minstrel sang in the Stó:lō longhouse of
the Lodge of Broken Bark.
Her lyrics spoke an oracle
of gifts from twelve nations of the world,
with crowns of twelve gemstones,
and the rivers of twelve oils
of the Holy Land.
My twelve poems
hailed the months of the year
in a garden called Earth,
watered by Rain.

Sextans

I.

When the ground is frosted,
harsh are the icicle eyelashes of January,
the honor of winter pierces the air
with cold and all that is left alone,
with frightening persuasion
left to die, emits its moan—
the sky wails with nothingness,
the lake is a frozen skyline,
a horizontal fault
whereupon the vertical line
reaches far into the earth.
The still red sun, note
the azure realm of predictable journeying.
Nocturnal are its depths,
deep and plumbed with
the accuracy and height of a totem.

Canada

II.

A gift from Canada,
I place in your hands a gold crown:
the stones are amber, fiery gems,
that speak of the iron and clay empire
and its royal virtue,
plunging your spirit into intimacy,
bearing your soul and your flag,
as a tree bears ripe fruit,
from its place of honor,
rooted deep within the ground.

From the top of the Hyssop River,
where you stand on the sacred mountain
your liturgy repeats:
"Wind, breathe in me.
Gate of the circlet of amber, open to me."

Taurus

I.

The garden of winter
sheds its soul in February, as a leaf
buds on the branch: first a bead
the size of a jewel, then the sweat
of the earth's natural pore emerges,
green and not gratuitous.
The rainbow moonstone shines through
the night emollient of winter
as a silver star would
if alone and without a friend,
as it breaks open to usher spring
slowly into color from white
and brightness from dark—
emanating beneath and pulsating through
the vast roots and branches of a tree
called the Milky Way.

Christmas Island

II.

A gift from Christmas Island,
I place in your hands a silver crown:
the stones are topaz, bright gems
that speak of the iron and clay empire
and its royal virtue,
plunging your spirit into intimacy,
bearing your soul and your flag
as a tree bears ripe fruit,
from its place of honor,
rooted deep within the ground.

From the top of the Aloe River,
where you stand on the sacred mountain
your liturgy speaks:
"Sea, chastise me with your fury.
Gate of the circlet of topaz, open to me."

Telescopium

I.

Blossoms cover the ground
as origami paper in March:
pale and translucent,
wanting a young planet to
decorate as an ode
to last governess,
demonstrative,
ordained,
the germination
of a thought
which grows in season—
then bursts forth,
pungent and afraid
of its own nectar,
the sting of bees,
and the sweetness of time.

Costa Rica

II.

A gift from Costa Rica,
I place in your hands a bronze crown:
the stones are citrine, fire-hued gems
that speak of the iron and clay empire
and its royal virtue,
plunging your spirit into intimacy,
bearing your soul and your flag
as a tree bears ripe fruit,
from its place of honor,
rooted deep within the ground.

From the top of the Spikenard river,
where you stand on the sacred mountain
your liturgy echoes:
"Salt, cleanse my wounds.
Gate of the circlet of citrine, open to me."

Triangulum

I.

The pearl flood
of April is a chaste gemstone
in the heart of spring,
lavishing the sky with
clear rain drops,
streaming down the windows,
drying as minerals
lucid in angel dust:
the guerdon of wheat fields
after frost, before the planting—
softening
as ghee in a saucepan.
The cook took its essence,
poured it into a jar,
wrapped it in tin foil,
used it sparingly.

II. Egypt

A gift from Egypt,
I place in your hands a copper crown:
the stones are emerald, glittering gems
that speak of the iron and clay empire
and its royal virtue,
plunging your spirit into intimacy,
bearing your soul and your flag
as a tree bears ripe fruit,
from its place of honor,
rooted deep within the ground.

From the top of the Myrtle River,
where you stand on the sacred mountain,
your liturgy resounds:
"Sand, number my thoughts.
Gate of the circlet of emerald, open to me."

Triangulum Australe

I.

The bright song went forth
in May as a popular hit
recording of an old favorite, classic
and vibrant, resonating in store windows,
reverberating on vintage turntables,
dumbfounded with rustic charm:
the arms of life stretched
out to the rays of sun,
emanating heat of the burning
bright star,
boiling water on the sidewalk,
making joggers wear yoga pants,
Lululemonites
climbing Grouse Mountain.
Women should speak up
for themselves, they said.

II.

Great Britain

A gift from Great Britain,
I place in your hands an iron crown:
the stones are sapphire, prophetic gems
that speak of the iron and clay empire
and its royal virtue,
plunging your spirit into intimacy,
bearing your soul and your flag
as a tree bears ripe fruit,
from its place of honor,
rooted deep within the ground.

From the top of the Galbanum River,
where you stand on the sacred mountain
you cried out:
"Trees, surround me with protection.
Gate of the circlet of sapphire, open to me."

Tucana

I.

The early summer was guarded and reticent
in June, the earth cracking as if on a seismic
fault line, donning a crisp cucumber
and avocado mask.
The gust of wind dried the desert to flame
opened a paradox of Pandora's box,
watching dolphins play at sea
as children do kiss,
praying on their knees
before off to bed.
The graphic or figurative
earthen pots of a coral palace,
all uniform as the stars
and terra-cotta, shaped
voluntarily as olive trees grow,
the lead mass of a kiln.

II. Israel

A gift from Israel,
I place in your hands a white gold crown:
the stones are amethyst, purple gems
that speak of the iron and clay empire
and its royal virtue.
Plunging your spirit into intimacy,
bearing your soul and your flag
as a tree bears ripe fruit,
from its place of honor,
rooted deep within the ground.

From the top of the Helisynchrum River,
where you stand on the sacred mountain
your liturgy speaks:
"Air, fill my lungs.
Gate of the circlet of amethyst, open to me."

Ursa Major

I.

The movement of sun
from morning to the end of July,
as the scale crescendos from one end of the keyboard
to the other: note upon note,
each a fragment of sound, fury,
and color. The pianist, silent at each
rest, diminutive in pianissimo,
an accent of thunder over the sea,
ever-changing light in piano, waves
in forte, and staccato of the rain.
The puddles recorded the sound,
the basin called earth produced
a record of its majesty:
sonata in D major,
evaluating the sea hills' amplitude,
reverberating into acknowledgement.

II. Mozambique

A gift from Mozambique,
I place in your hands a rose gold crown:
the stones are chalcedony, bloodstone gems
that speak of the iron and clay empire
and its royal virtue,
plunging your spirit into intimacy,
bearing your soul and your flag
as a tree bears ripe fruit,
from its place of honor,
rooted deep within the ground.

From the top of the Onychra River,
where you stand on the sacred mountain
your liturgy sings:
"Light, illumine me to what is right.
Gate of the circlet of chalcedony, open to me."

Ursa Minor

I.

Raise the shades,
open the windows of August,
let the air blow through:
the mantle of an idea, a chasuble of summer
obscuring salty froth
as the sea hits the boardwalk with a cloak of spray,
effervescent as a Perrier on ice,
a contrive of finesse, polite and civil.
Dwelling place of my soul,
a mansion on a hilltop, resplendent
in darkening light, as the sun bends
and disappears, trees reaching like shadows,
faintly tinged with traditional night,
the corporeal dwelling of a collection of artifacts,
at last, drawing its velvet curtain:
the hall of leniency, the seat of orthodoxy.

II. New Zealand

A gift from New Zealand,
I place in your hands a coral crown:
the stones are aquamarine, sparkling gems
that speak of the iron and clay empire
and its royal virtue,
plunging your spirit into intimacy,
bearing your soul and your flag
as a tree bears ripe fruit,
from its place of honor,
rooted deep within the ground.

From the top of the Cistus River,
where you stand on the sacred mountain
your liturgy is repeated:
"Dark, forgive my fear.
Gate of the circlet of aquamarine, open to me."

Vela

I.

The quiet road
unfolding from September,
like the manifold purpose of the divine:
a first idea, then logic,
followed by a row of houses,
the paved street of a human heart,
with arteries and veins of gold—
no equal mythic course.
In the midnight of solitude,
translucent of the confines, reticent and real—
if these lights be angels, they shall light the way;
both strong in the dark and stormy-eyed,
the courageous and dignified response
to the prodigality of a rival,
beating wings, bearing farewells
with maternal revelation.

II. Peru

A gift from Peru,
I place in your hands an ivory crown:
the stones are agate, molten gems
that speak of the iron and clay empire
and its royal virtue,
plunging your spirit into intimacy,
bearing your soul and your flag
as a tree bears ripe fruit,
from its place of honor,
rooted deep within the ground.

From the top of the Myrrh River,
where you stand on the sacred mountain
your liturgy prays silently:
"Rain, I will go to the lost.
Gate of the circlet of agate, open to me."

Virgo

I.

Intersecting with the calm
October winds of Abbotsford,
the reflection of light,
a meditation of stillness,
a frequency of color and sound,
emanating from the menial to the logistic,
born to the world of archangels and demons,
an intellectual break with time and place,
resonant truism or rebel realist.
I saw my mother bend
with the blue and white sari of a sun-cast land,
stirring the aspens from fervor to casual breezes;
the gewgaw of planets and haloes of moons
in the museum of the galaxy,
glass beads threaded
as the meteors of her necklace.

II. Scotland

A gift from Scotland,
I place in your hands an ebony crown:
the stones are carnelian, brocade gems
that speak of the iron and clay empire
and its royal virtue,
plunging your spirit into intimacy,
bearing your soul and your flag
as a tree bears ripe fruit,
from its place of honor,
rooted deep within the ground.

From the top of the Cypress River,
where you stand on the sacred mountain
your liturgy resonates:
"Fruit, nourish me.
Gate of the circlet of carnelian, open to me."

Volans

I.

Descant into the fray, unable to stifle
the meandering November like a mastered fable,
incredulous at purpose and rhyme:
if these poets be gods, then god-like create—
our first stones at Goliaths, hurled, matchless
and exquisite to oppose
an army of poverty and injustice.
Marshall the token note,
buttress the Longfellow of faded parchment,
his lacy script, lazing into society with eye-catching
contrast, a dying swan against the lake—
obsessed with perfection,
the flawless performance of virtue,
a principal on dexterous ground,
sculpted by the master in the tradition of the elect,
standing proud in the gallery of time.

II. United States

A gift from the United States,
I place in your hands a crystal crown:
the stones are midnight onyx, glowing gems
that speak of the iron and clay empire
and its royal virtue,
plunging your spirit into intimacy,
bearing your soul and your flag
as a tree bears ripe fruit,
from its place of honor,
rooted deep within the ground.

From the top of the Frankincense river,
where you stand on the sacred mountain
your liturgy resounds:
Life, be the strength I profess.
Gate of the circlet of midnight onyx, open to me.

Vulpecula

I.

In the perplexing way
of a rugged bite of December landscape,
freezing the horizon with a first hint of light,
philosophizing unity with morning,
pondering the ethnic medicine,
rivaling the oils of elders,
an advocate nutrient be physic of the spare.
The apex of harmony, a colorful companion
from head to foot—the sun will rise again
in the spring, and water will flow like
a balm down the mountain.
Where is the home of the palm, the fig, and the date?
Sugary and succulent fruit melting
on the tree; be it sweetness
when the government doesn't make sense,
a shiny penny is left, a token for your thoughts.

II. Vatican City

A gift from Vatican City,
I place in your hands a platinum crown:
the stones are garnet, cardinal gems
that speak of the iron and clay empire
and its royal virtue,
plunging your spirit into intimacy,
bearing your soul and your flag
as a tree bears ripe fruit,
from its place of honor,
rooted deep within the ground.

From the top of the Cassia river,
where you stand on the sacred mountain
your liturgy would not recant:
"Death, be the gate I pass through.
Gate of the circlet of Christ, open to me."

Epilogue

It was after the frost, when the rivers
burgeon with snowmelt,
and the deer come down the mountain,
that I made my way
to the longhouse beside the Fraser River.

I presented Raven with two paintings
on parchment,
signed by Sea and Rain
of fruits and flowers at the end
of the smudging ceremony.
The twelve elders gave us
their blessing.
Raven returned the next morning
to her cabin and
the shores of Long Beach.

Although I lived a full life,
and did not die of cancer,
it was my relationship to the Stó:lō people
and the medicine woman, Naiya
that cemented my life force
to the four medicines,
the four seasons, and the four directions.
It was the minstrel and Wen
who had secured my heart
for an eternal home.

It was true in the end,
that the sea could not die, but live.
Repelling all unrest, illness and disease,
it is a restless body of salt
beneath the sky.

Table 1.0 Healing Appendix

Color	Organ	Virtue	Essential oil	Gemstone/metal
Gold	Adrenal glands	Kindness	Hyssop	Gold
Silver	Thyroid gland	Purity	Balsam	Silver
Bronze	Pituitary gland	Chivalry	Tansy	Bronze
Copper	Gonadal glands	Dignity	Aloe	Copper
Iron	Hypothalamus	Fortitude	Spikenard	Iron
Clay	Parathyroid gland	Healing	Myrtle	Crystal
Red	Heart	Love	Cinnamon	Amber
Orange	Pancreas	Generosity	Orange	Topaz
Yellow	Lymphatic system	Tolerance	Citronella	Citrine
Green	Liver	Patience	Clary sage	Emerald
Blue	Lungs	Joy	Eucalyptus	Sapphire
Purple	Muscles	Goodness	Lavender	Amethyst
Brown	Large intestines	Practicality	Cedar	Bernadine
Black	Kidneys	Self control	Anise	Black onyx
White	Brain	Peace	Camphor	Cubic zirconia
Clear	Immune System	Artistry	Melissa	Diamond
Pink	Reproductive system	Grace	Rosehip	Tourmaline
Peach	Skin	Thankful	Jasmine	Morganite
Burgundy	Joints	Strength	Ledum	Spinel
Lime	Gallbladder	Warmth	Tarragon	Peridot
Chocolate	Small Intestine	Integrity	Nutmeg	Tiger's Eye
Navy	Hair & Nails	Discretion	Fennel	Aquamarine
Ivory	Bones	Sincerity	Helisynchrum	Ivory
Beige	Stomach	Serenity	Juniper	Mother-of-pearl
Dark Green	Detox System	Prudence	Oregano	Jasper
Cream	Nervous System	Resourceful	Onychra	Pearl
Crimson	Red Blood Cell	Devotion	Geranium	Ruby
Scarlet	Spleen	Gentleness	Bergamot	Carnelian
Turquoise	Cell	Friendship	Petit grain	Lapis lazuli
Sunshine	Arms & legs	Brilliance	Lemonbalm	Sphene
Coffee	Appendix	Forgiveness	Clove	Champagne diamond
Violet	Diaphragm	Faith	Tsuga	Chalcedony
Light Blue	Pharynx	Intellect	Spearmint	Rainbow moonstone
Khaki	Nose & sinus	Orderly	Peppermint	Jade
Fuchsia	Mouth	Healthy	Myrrh	Zircon
Moss	Sphincters	Modesty	Holy basil	Apatite
Pewter	Bladder	Humility	Cypress	Agate
Opal	Eggs/Sperm	Qualified	Ylang ylang	Opal

Steel	Hands & feet	Industrious	Pine	Smoky quartz
Magenta	Mammary glands	Nourishing	Frankincense	Garnet
Marine	Embryo	Persevering	Pepper	Midnight onyx
Mauve	Bodily Fluids	Obedient	Rose	Hyacinth
Sable	Teeth/gums	Stable	Sandalwood	Cameo onyx
Coral	Animals	Balanced	Ginger	Coral
Sunrise	Eyes	Clarity	Lemon	Chrysoberyl
Sunset	Ears	Clean	Tea tree	Fire opal